which?
essential guides

ONEY
VING
NDBOOK

D1579333

" This book should save you money, but not by involving you in complications or risks. It consists of tried-and-tested ideas – and it tells you how not to lose your hard-earned money as well. **"**

Tony Levene

About the author

Tony Levene has been a financial writer for over three decades specialising in personal finance. He has worked for a number of national newspapers, including *The Sunday Times* and *Daily Express*. He is the author of several books including *Tax Handbook* (an annual publication in the *Which? Essential Guides* series), *How to Win in the Insurance Jungle* and *The Shares Game*. He has worked for *Guardian Money* since 1998. Tony lives in London with Claudia, grown-up children Zoë and Oliver, and cats Plato, Pandora and Pascal.

MONEY
SAVING
HANDBOOK

TONY LEVENE

Which? Books are commissioned and published by Which? Ltd,
2 Marylebone Road, London NW1 4DF
Head of Which? Books: Angela Newton
Project management for Which? Books: Claudia Dyer
Email: books@which.co.uk

Distributed by Littlehampton Book Services Ltd, Faraday Close, Durrington, Worthing,
West Sussex BN13 3RB

British Library Cataloguing in Publication Data
A catalogue record for this book is available from the British Library

ISBN 978 1 84490 048 0

1 3 5 7 9 10 8 6 4 2

Author's acknowledgements
The author would like to acknowledge the forebearance of his colleagues at *The
Guardian*, the contribution of its readers, and the invaluable help of Which? research.

Edited by: Emma Callery
Designed by: Bob Vickers
Index by: Lynda Swindells
Cover photographs by: Getty (left); Alamy (right)
Printed and bound by VivaPress, Barcelona, Spain

Arctic Volume White is an elemental chlorine-free paper produced at Arctic Paper
Hafrestroms AB in Åsensbruk, Sweden, using timber from sustainably managed forests.
The mill is ISO14001 and EMAS certified, and has PEFC and FSC certified Chain of
Custody.

Contents

Introduction

The art of saving money is knowing how to spend less but end up with the same as others who lay out a whole lot more cash. It needs care, discipline and a measure of self-control, but the effort is worthwhile – you'll end up with more for less and at the same time you could have lower debts or owe nothing.

Look after the pennies and the pounds will look after themselves. Or is it 'penny wise, pound foolish'? The English language is full of proverbs that offer two opposing views of life. And money savers can take their choice. The first route is central to the *Which? Essential Guide Money Saving Handbook*. This philosophy takes as its starting point the concept that sensible economies and money saving techniques can easily lead to greater things.

❝ There are times when making economies can be counter-productive, ending up wasting both money and time. ❞

DON'T BE PENNY WISE BUT POUND FOOLISH

It is, however, all too easy to fall into the 'penny wise, pound foolish' camp where you end up spending a few pennies less but at a cost. You can effectively 'beat yourself up' to make economies and this can be counter-productive, wasting money and time rather than saving money. Some examples will make this clear.

Borrowing big sums on a succession of 0 per cent credit cards is getting tougher now although it is still possible. It can be worthwhile juggling cards if the alternative is to pay 15 or 20 per cent or even more in interest. But the advice given by some to borrow at 0 per cent and then invest the money in a savings account may not always be that worthwhile. The effort and discipline

 Information about using credit cards responsibly and efficiently is given on pages 60-8 and shopping for everyday items is covered on pages 147-62.

incurred are considerable. Furthermore, if you were to follow this line but made a mistake with a repayment or it is a single day late, then credit card companies jump up and down with glee as their small print may then allow them to hit you with all sorts of charges, more than wiping out your gains. One more thing – many of the figures quoted in this advice fail to mention the tax you'll probably have to pay on your savings interest.

Similarly, you can save money while out shopping for everyday items if you always aim for the low-cost goods. But is this always the best course? Many comparison tables of supermarket prices, for instance, ignore 'quality'. It is pointless buying low-cost foods that are so inedible that you throw them all away. Some 'value' clothes last well – they are cheap because they are simple items that can be mass-produced and you are not paying for the privilege of a well-advertised brand name. But others shrink or fall apart after just one wearing and washing. On a personal note, I once tried to save money with an economy cat food. My cats uniformly turned up their feline noses and refused to touch the stuff, which had to be thrown away. A total waste of money.

It is rare that a single day goes past without spending money on something. Often, our purses, wallets and plastic cards may be in action a dozen or more times in 24 hours. It is all too easy to lose control of spending – especially as so much of commerce today is designed to make us less responsible in our use of money. On a basic level, this book looks at the tricks supermarket owners use to make us spend more than we otherwise would – or would need to. This can include the obvious placing of sweets by the checkout to the subtle positioning of higher cost items at eye level leaving you to bend down or stretch upwards to get at the better value goods.

This book aims to make you both penny wise and pound wise. It does this in two ways.

“Making a mistake with a repayment or even being a single day late allows credit card companies to hit you with all sorts of charges.”

MAKE BETTER SPENDING DECISIONS

The first key step towards saving money is to make better spending decisions while ending up with the same outcomes as the higher cost alternative.

The internet with its almost infinite amount of information is the best place to start. The first chapter looks at how and where to get information, including the strengths (and weaknesses) of price-comparison sites. You can compare everything from the price of a CD to the cost of your life insurance. But even if you are a computer-phobe or a computer-illiterate, don't worry.

Increasingly, companies are aware of the online pricing information and they know many of their potential customers will look at this so they adjust their prices downwards. You would still be better off, however, doing your own research on major items – you can't rely on any firm, no matter how good a brand name it has.

There are then chapters that look at:

- **Major financial items,** such as home loans, home and car insurances, life cover and bank accounts. There are amazing savings between the best and the worst buy – and there is often no difference for the consumer in what they receive.
- **Which insurance schemes** are good value and those, such as extended warranty or payment protection insurance, that should be shunned as a waste of your cash.
- **Holidays, travel costs** and whether you are better off buying a package deal or putting it altogether yourself.
- **How to make sense of smaller spending items,** which can add up to big savings. Check out the sections on mobile and landline phones, broadband and energy costs.
- **Ways to save tax,** including getting your boss to help you buy a bike, as well as a legitimate method of avoiding tax on your savings interest.

AVOID LOSING MONEY

The second strand in the *Money Saving Handbook* is how to avoid being conned out of your money. There is obviously no point putting a considerable amount of effort into saving money if you then lose it the first time you run into someone determined to take more of your cash

> **&& The key step towards saving money is to make better spending decisions. For this you need reliable information rather than relying on the brand name. 99**

 Use online comparison sites to enhance your money saving abilities - see pages 17-22 for the up- and downsides of the internet.

Sale of Goods Act, 2003

When you shop – whether in person, by post, by phone or on the internet – you have substantial legal rights under the Sale of Goods Act, 2003. When you buy a product, it must:

- Be of satisfactory quality and conform to safety legislation. It should not have faults (even minor blemishes) unless it is sold as 'damaged' or 'shop-soiled'. Goods that are unsafe, such as electrical goods with bare wires, must not be sold under any circumstances.
- Be durable. Goods should stand up to reasonable wear and tear.
- Be fit for the purpose. An umbrella should keep the rain off, not let it leak through holes.
- Match the description.

If you have a problem:

- You can demand a full refund provided you do this speedily (usually within two to three weeks). Stores should not fob you off with a replacement or a credit note.
- If you discover the fault within six months, the shop has to prove the fault did not exist at the time of purchase.

- You may be entitled to some recompense if a fault comes to light within six years (five in Scotland), although this will depend on the reasonable durability and nature of the goods.
- Despite what you may be told, you do NOT need your receipt (although a proof of purchase makes life easier for you).

You have no legal right to complain if you break something through misuse or if you change your mind on perfectly good items, although many stores will offer a refund, replacement or credit note to maintain customer goodwill.

The staff of some retailers may try to deny these rights exist. You do not have to deal with the manufacturer yourself (although this may sometimes be easier) because your contract is with the retailer, not the manufacturer. So always stand your ground, and be prepared to make a formal complaint to the store's head office. If that fails, contact Consumer Direct (see page 206) or your local trading standards department.

Money saving tips

Throughout this book, there are 'money saving tips', which show how cutting back or giving up relatively small purchases can add up to big money over a year. These are all tried and tested! They will work better if you set yourself a target for your savings – and promise yourself a treat for all the hard work and deprivation!

than you need to spend. With this in mind, the book tells you how to:

- Protect yourself in a home improvement transaction – the gap between good value and what you would pay to an unscrupulous salesperson for the same new kitchen can easily top £5,000. Go for the more expensive deal and you are literally throwing what it took you months to earn down the drain. Not a pretty sight.
- Avoid being taken for a ride when you buy a car. There is a simple strategy that can knock a fair slice off the 'sticker' price the vehicle displays on the forecourt.
- Avoid being exploited again with an over-priced finance package.
- Avoid falling for 'scams'. Designed to keep you from falling foul of some of the amazing ways scamsters have developed to separate you from everything, starting with £10 and running up to £10,000.

THE MONEY SAVER'S ABC

Finally, there is an extended list of organisations that offer advice and help. Besides giving internet sites, addresses and phone numbers (where applicable), this last chapter tells you what these organisations do (and sometimes don't do).

WHAT THIS BOOK CANNOT DO

No book can give up-to-date prices or the 'terms and conditions' (the T&C, which does not mean tenderness and care!) that companies impose on deals and often change, giving whatever the legal minimum notice might be in each instance.

But Which? can. Check out the Which? website (www.which.co.uk) and the monthly *Which?* and *Which? Money* magazines. These give information on constantly changing prices and deals.

And finally don't forget that the flipside of saving money is to spend it on something enjoyable and worthwhile. There is something sad about someone dying who leaves an estate worth £500,000 or more who spent the last 30 years of his or her life existing on budget sliced white bread and the cheapest margarine. Not wasting money can mean more to spend on others, giving to charity – and treating yourself!

"The flipside of saving money is that you can spend it on something enjoyable and worthwhile, like a treat, a friend or a charity."

The switching game

There are literally tens of thousands of financial possibilities in everything from mortgages to mobile phones. This chapter looks at information sources that tell you how to separate your personal wheat from the chaff – a vital first step in saving money. It also weighs up whether switching or sticking with product providers is the best course.

It pays to shop around

You can't 'kick the tyres' when you buy insurance, loans, electricity or bank accounts in the same way as you would when purchasing tangible items such as a car. That makes it far more difficult to judge value for money. Finding your way through the price jungle is the essential first step to saving money. But just where do you start?

Buying a consumer item is easy. You decide on a budget – perhaps anything from £20 to £20,000 if you are buying a watch – and go to the right sort of shop. For the cheaper watch, you would look at market stalls, supermarkets, chain stores or online sites. Buying the top-price model would require a visit to a luxury jeweller. If you were in a position to make this choice, you would know that while both price levels would give you a watch that tells the time, the cheaper one is probably made of plastic while the expensive one is more likely to be diamond encrusted solid gold.

Buying an item such as a DVD or CD is different although equally easy. Once you have decided on the title you want, you have a choice of either going online to find the cheapest supplier, perhaps filling in complicated credit card details and then waiting a few days for delivery, or heading off to the nearest high street retailer where you can take instant delivery and pay cash if you wish. But wherever you go, you know that the contents of the box will be identical – the decision is based on price and convenience.

> **&& Buying standard items such as a DVD or CD comes down to price and convenience. Other product choices also have a quality element. &&**

 You can shop around by taking to the streets, picking up the phone, using a broker or going online. There are pros and cons to each of these - they are covered over pages 13-22.

Buying a financial item is far more difficult. There are huge numbers of products, which all claim to fulfil the same basic need, such as insuring your home or lending you £2,000. Often, the only discernible difference between them is price not quality. You could easily be quoted £1,200, £1,000, £800, £600 or even £400 for insurance to cover the same property. Two weeks' travel insurance in Europe for two adults and two children might cost £30 or more than five times that amount, depending on where and how you buy it. And that £2,000 personal loan could cost you anything from 6.9 per cent to a mouth-watering 172 per cent.

Your purchase decision on a financial item is likely to be driven solely by price – there are usually other factors to take into account, but what you pay is nearly always the main reason for choosing one insurance policy or loan over another.

The problem with searching out a good buy in this particular way is that you cannot walk up and down the local shopping mall and compare prices in the shop windows.

You probably would not want to, either. In contrast to shopping for a new watch or the latest film or music, most of the items in the *Money Saving Handbook* are known as 'distress purchases' – you have

to buy them whether you like it or not. Motor insurance, which is compulsory, and buildings insurance, which is obligatory if you have a mortgage, are two examples.

There are a number of routes to finding the basic pricing information you need to make a money saving decision.

❝ Buying a financial item or a 'distress purchase' is difficult. You can't compare them in shop windows, and there are so many products to vet. ❞

TAKING TO THE STREETS

You could literally pound the streets from bank to bank, from phone shop to phone shop, from insurance broker to insurance broker to find the best deals. What you do here effectively is to select the firms that you might wish to do business with first – if only because they are the ones you come across in your travels – and then ask what they can do for you (see the pros and cons chart, overleaf).

 Insuring your home is covered in detail on pages 83-5 and travel insurance is explained on pages 78-9.

The pros and cons of face-to-face contact

Pros

- You get to see the organisation you are dealing with face-to-face and you discuss your needs with a real person. This can be useful because it enables you to make a first-impressions judgement on the firm. Was the person you saw in the flesh welcoming or dismissive? Was the phone line you called to make an appointment answered swiftly or did you have to wait an eternity listening to music you would not have chosen?

- You can be accurate in stating your exact needs. Each of us is an individual with specific requirements. The person who fields your enquiry should be able either to create a product that fits in with what you want or tell you that you should try elsewhere for something more suitable.

- You can ask all sorts of questions – and judge the organisation on how it responds to you (open? clear? evasive? confusing?). At this stage the company wants you as a paying customer, but how will it react if there is a problem or you need to claim on the insurance policy it wants you to buy? It's better to make a judgement now rather than discovering the firm is customer unfriendly when you need something from it.

- At the end of each fact-finding you will be able to collect a definite quote in writing or have one sent to you. These will usually be good for 30 days so you have time to collect a number and make comparisons.

- You may find that talking directly with someone produces a solution to your needs that you had not thought of.

Cons

- This process can be very time consuming. Expect an enquiry for home insurance to last 15–30 minutes, one for car insurance to take up 10 minutes. And that does not count time you might have to wait.

- You may have to make an appointment beforehand to discuss a product face-to-face on the high street as the interview process for complex products such as life insurance may take an hour or longer.

- Some organisations keep strict 9am to 5pm Monday to Friday hours, which may not suit you.

- Only a proportion of lenders, insurers or other financial providers have easy-to-find high street outlets so you could miss out on a large slice of the market. This is a major disadvantage as many financial companies with good value products have almost no consumer recognition since they are not famous brands.

- You may be talked into unsuitable products by financial company employees who are paid on commission.

- It is always harder to say 'no' in a face-to-face interview than over the phone or online. The earnings of the salesperson will depend on sales success and they are trained in getting you to put your signature on the bottom of an agreement.

DIALLING FOR INFORMATION

You can get information at the end of a phone line – the numbers are usually available from adverts or from internet sites. This has a number of similarities with the face-to-face approach (see the pros and cons charts, opposite and below). Some firms only operate at the end of a phone line.

> **"** A broker will know the market, and you can check their status through the FSA register. **"**

USING A BROKER

Instead of going directly to a company, you go to a broker who knows the market and can sell products from many, if not all, of the firms active in the market. Many brokers in areas such as mortgages, loans and insurance are local and often concentrate on face-to-face advice. You can find brokers either from adverts or local Yellow Pages – but a good source is the www.unbiased.co.uk site, which will give you local independent financial advisers. You can also check on the status of a broker through the Financial Services Authority (FSA) register (see overleaf).

The pros and cons of phone centre contact

Pros	Cons
• You can take in more firms in a given length of time.	• Complicated plans can be difficult to understand - both they and you can make mistakes.
• You don't generally have to make an appointment.	• It is harder to judge an organisation on a phone line than face-to-face.
• It is easier to say no - by terminating the call if necessary.	• Call centre staff are often incentivised to deal with the maximum number of customers possible in an hour so you may be rushed into making a decision.
• You have a greater choice of firms.	

 The website for the Financial Services Authority (FSA) register is: www.fsa.gov.uk. See also page 208 for further infromation about the FSA.

The pros and cons of using a broker

Pros

- A broker should be able to offer advice on a wide range of products from many if not all the providers in the market – unlike the high street bank, which concentrates on one range.
- Local brokers have local knowledge – invaluable in being aware of special deals for your area, such as in motor insurance, where some firms specialise in rural areas and others go for city centres; in mortgages where some lenders prefer a certain locality (perhaps a close radius to its headquarters) while others will not lend in some areas (such as the Scottish highlands and islands).
- Brokers tend to be entrepreneurial – it's in their interest to find something to match your needs rather than send you away with a 'computer says no' approach. If you are a 17-year-old with a Ferrari, you'll be turned down flat as uninsurable by high street firms and call centres alike. But brokers know there is always some firm that will take on the risk for a suitable premium. In the same way, brokers can find lenders prepared to take on someone with an appalling credit record, but at a price!
- Brokers often have high levels of expertise in the market as a whole – they are not tied-in by one company's way of thinking.
- Deals may be better than you can get by going direct to the product provider – investment brokers may rebate part of the commission while some may be able to offer better mortgages than the mortgage company itself because their costs are lower.
- Brokers should help you if you have a problem or a claim.

Cons

- Brokers can be slow – you are dependent on the broker and the broker has to wait for the product provider. Many systems have been updated and most brokers use the internet to speed matters up. But you cannot necessarily expect a quick decision, especially if your requirements are complicated.
- Product bias – you may be pushed towards an investment, loan, mortgage or insurance that pays the broker more than other rival products with a similar profile, even if this is not the best advice for you. So you may end up with the wrong mortgage while enriching the broker.
- You may not be advised on a course of action, even though it would be best for you, because it will earn the broker nothing. You are also unlikely to be pointed towards basic advice that is available at no charge or towards sources of products that are simple to apply. Bad advice will cost you money, while not taking wrong advice will save you money.
- Fees – some brokers charge you even though they may also collect a commission from the product company. For instance, on investment products known as insurance bonds, brokers can take as much as 7 per cent. You could also find you are paying a fee to a mortgage broker for a home loan that you could find fee-free on the high street or online. Always ask the broker to explain what he or she is providing that you couldn't get elsewhere for free. In general, brokers should account for everything they earn in the way of commission from the product provider. They can offset this against any agreed fees, but often they will only carry out this money saving manoeuvre if you demand it.

ONLINE COMPARISON SITES

This is the fastest growing area of the advice market with new sites regularly appearing. It's not hard to understand why. These often cover hard-to-compare areas such as utilities – gas, electricity, phone and broadband connections – which may have no high street outlets and where brokers are non-existent and where products did not really exist a decade or so ago. Of course, they also cover conventional products, such as mortgages, insurances, loans, pensions and savings accounts. Millions of people look at these sites each month.

All-encompassing sites: Websites you find through publicity or personal recommendation generally ask you to fill in an online form and submit it. The comparison site then contacts all potential insurance companies and requests a quote for you, based on your details. A few seconds or minutes (depending on the site) later, you receive an email or see a new screen that lists what the site considers to be the best value providers for your needs. You can then view the policy details for each quote, make any changes you might want and buy the policy – or save it and come back later.

The middle man: A variation on the all-encompassing sites is to ask customers to fill in a very basic form for insurance and then point you towards the most suitable insurers for you, based on price and the type of cover you need. It is then up to you whether you visit the suggested insurers' own sites and ask for quotations. These will normally involve completing a far longer form.

Whichever type of site you use, it is then your choice either to go ahead and sign yourself up (if it is a relatively simple product whose sale is not especially regulated, such as broadband or gas or electricity), receive further details (necessary for complex, regulated products such as mortgages) or abandon the search.

Most comparison sites are run by commercial companies, which earn money if your online enquiry turns into a decision to buy. So if you change your gas or electricity supplier as a result of an online decision, the comparison site picks up around £40–£50 from the new company. Some comparison sites earn smaller sums on 'click-throughs', payments made when you enquire further about a firm's products, regardless of whether you buy or not.

The comparison sites are useful tools – but you do have to be aware of their limitations, which are described overleaf.

Some useful comparison sites to visit are www.which.co.uk, www.unbiased.co.uk (the website for IFA Promotion), and www.impartial.com.

The pros and cons of using an online comparison site

Pros

- Online sites are – or should be – continually updated so they are the only place where consumers can find current information and best buys from a large number of sources with just one computer form to fill in.
- Sites will generally retain your details – if you want – so you can come back a day or a week later and not have to start all over again.

Cons

- If you're going to use a comparison site as anything more than a first base for research, then you're leaving it up to a third party to find the best deal, and a third party will never go as far as you can. It's not in their interests to get every customer the very best deal, nor is it possible when looking at complex matters such as insurance.
- Price isn't always everything. Comparison sites do not allow you to check the quality of what is on offer.
- An online site might not be independent.
- Providers can pay to appear in a comparison table.
- There can be hidden costs.
- You might not be able to take advantage of the offer.
- The sites might not be comprehensive.
- The sites display the same information in different ways.
- The sites might not be accurate.
- Sites are only individualised up to a certain point.

An online site might not be independent

All sites claim to be independent and bias free. If they did not make this claim, they would be automatically dismissed as worthless. But there can be questions over their impartiality because some are owned by companies that also provide insurance or other financial products as well as information on their rivals. As a result, it is unclear how such sites deal with the conflicts that must arise on the occasions when their own products are far from being the best buys.

Some sites are also controversial because they charge product providers a fixed monthly fee if they wish their details to be included, irrespective of the size of the financial company. This may mean that smaller product providers may not appear on certain sites as they judge the sum demanded too great for the amount of business generated, creating a bias towards bigger companies.

66 Setting up three credit cards could result in being given lower spending limits, or a generous limit tripled. 99

Websites can be too clever for your own good!

Another site may point you towards three credit cards – one for purchases, one for transferring debts on other cards you have built up in the past, and one for overseas use. Although this would get the site three fees, this can have money saving merits if you can juggle the three cards. But whether the three cards indicated are best for you as an individual is not obvious and nor will the site warn you that applying and being accepted for three cards at once could result in you getting a far lower spending limit on each one – or the danger of getting a generous limit multiplied by three, which

Ask the expert

How can I tell if a site is independent?

The simple answer is that you can't because some companies pay fees to appear on comparison sites, which are not subject to any disclosure rules. But you can help yourself by always looking at more than one site.

You may notice names that are in some lists while being absent from others. The ones that are missing are not necessarily good or bad buys – it may simply be that the product providers decide to pay to be on one site and not another.

There have been allegations (roundly denied) that some sites favour companies that pay them higher commissions. While no site will openly tell users about these, you can often tell by looking for signs such as highlighted products followed by a 'you can apply for this NOW!' label. Other sites use phrases such as 'best selling' or 'pick of our buys', which do not mean that they are the best products for your particular circumstances. A further variant is to label some products as 'sponsored links'.

Don't feel that you automatically have to reject these products – simply be aware that the site is trying to persuade you towards them for its own commercial reasons.

may tempt you into spending but which you may not be able to service when it comes to interest and repayment.

Providers can pay to appear in a comparison table

On products such as credit cards, once you have decided which type of card you want, you are taken to another page for the results of the search, with cards ranked in order of their suitability. Once again you need to proceed with care. The most prominent 'results' you see on the page may be from providers that have paid to appear on the comparison tables (see 'Ask the expert' on page 19).

For example, if you were searching for a card with the lowest interest rate on **balance transfers** for the **life of balance**, the best option might be the card that charges 4.9 per cent until the balance is repaid. But it might only appear on the results page below sponsored links for other cards, both of which have higher interest rates.

There can be hidden costs

A site may not be able to tell you if your application will be dealt with at the headline interest rate shown or if you will have to pay more. Look out for 'typical **APR**' on a listing. This means that only two-thirds of applicants are guaranteed to get this rate – regulatory rules only allow the use of a phrase such as 'typical rate' if at least 66.6 per cent are offered this level or lower. But if you're in the other 33.3 per cent you could pay substantially more – and that hardly saves money!

❝ Providers of the most prominent 'results' on a website page could have paid for their presence there. **❞**

Jargon buster

APR (Annual Percentage Rate) A formula set by the Office of Fair Trading which ensures that all published percentages are calculated in the same way

Balance transfers Outstanding amounts on one credit card that you move to another

Life of balance The time you take to pay off any balance transfer

 The ins and outs of credit card usage is covered on pages 60–8.

You might not be able to take advantage of the offer

Many lenders offer deals that are only available to borrowers with a perfect credit history. It's cheaper for them to finance these offers as the risks are lower, which is why they are more competitive. It also has the benefit of making them look good on best-buy tables, despite many people being unable to take advantage.

But some sites do offer some form of 'credit profiling', giving you the chance to answer some credit questions to check your acceptability. This may save you time by steering you away from cards where there is no hope of acceptance although as no two card companies have the same requirements – it can vary from card to card within a bank – this profiling can only be a rough check.

Are the sites comprehensive?

The gas and electricity comparison tools on the majority of sites that offer such comparisons are generally seen as fairly reflecting the entire market. This is because they are accredited by Energywatch, which would not issue its approval if there were gaping holes in the coverage. There are also only a limited number of gas and electricity providers so it is easier to make comparisons. Although there are many energy sites they nearly all use the same software and take in the same information. Other areas might not be so comprehensive, however.

Information is displayed in different ways

Insurance and financial services sites do not – and do not pretend – to include the entire market. Each quotes the number of insurers that they include (from 30 to 45, although some insurers appear under different guises, using one name for direct sales on the phone and another for sales through brokers). As a rule of thumb, sites have quotes from companies that provide around three-quarters of the relevant insurance – motor or household. But that does not mean they have three-quarters of all quotes as they concentrate on signing up the bigger insurers for their systems. One of the UK's biggest motor insurers has refused to sign up for any site – it claims it would rather save on the fees the sites want and pass on the savings to consumers.

The sites might not be accurate

- Broadband and phone packages: The sites are probably at their most accurate when it comes to these comparisons, which are fixed irrespective of variables such as your age, occupation, marital status and past claims history. But you have to compare like with like so deals that last 18 months should not be confused with those with a 12-month lifespan.
- Gas and electricity: These quotes should be accurate provided you have submitted your actual usage. One difficulty is whether past usage is an accurate measure of present or future consumption – you need to look at the

entire year, but bear in mind that one winter can be colder or warmer than normal. In addition, know that this month's best buy may not remain as next month's table topper. When energy prices were rising steeply in 2005 and 2006, some suppliers would aim to be the cheapest on the comparison sites, take in many new customers who were switching, and then increase bills substantially.

- **Insurance quotes:** Unlike face-to-face or phone conversations, comparison sites cannot pose such detailed questions, nor do they have access to the inner workings of the way different insurers assess risk. One insurer, for instance, may treat all shop workers as belonging to the same category. A second might differentiate between department stores, food shops and do-it-yourself superstores.

There are many true stories of quotes being wildly wrong. But in general, the prices they give fairly mirror the information that is inputted. If nothing else, they should give some indication as to which insurer is cheap and which expensive. It is always useful to have a rough idea of what the market is charging.

The problem of no or low choice

Areas where there are one or two dominant companies provide a problem for comparison sites because you then either get a long list of totally useless products or, as we show here, the whole thing is biased towards products from providers who pay for a high-level listing. As an example, one site has highlighted a particular bank account as a best buy for students, even though the account only goes up to 21 (when most students study for a year or two longer in their first degrees), does not have the automatic overdraft that most students need, does not have any on-campus branches and demands a regular monthly minimum. Even the bank itself does not advertise this as a student account. It is, in fact, an account for 18–21-year-olds who decide to take up full-time paid employment for whom it could be a best buy. Another account on the same listing only applies to those under 19 – almost worthless for most university students.

Why are these accounts on the recommended list? It seems that whoever compiled the information did so on the basis of how much the account paid in interest on amounts in credit. This only applies to a minority of students, as most are in debt to their bank.

Sites are only individualised up to a point

They can never cover most of the people most of the time and they can become unreliable – or they will refuse to quote – if you have requirements that are less ordinary. For instance, they do not work for people with severe credit problems who are looking for a mortgage or someone who has suffered serious illnesses who needs life insurance.

The Financial Services Authority (FSA)

Most comparison sites are commercial and have substantial advertising budgets to attract users. One site that does not advertise itself very often – and one that does not earn from anyone following its information – is the Financial Services Authority's own comparison site at www.moneymadeclear.fsa.gov.uk, which promises you 'impartial information, no selling, no jargon, just the facts'.

The site offers generic information on a number of financial areas including savings accounts, investment-based individual savings accounts, investment bonds, endowments, mortgages, stakeholder pensions and annuities. More importantly, it also offers comparative tables for the first five products in each category so you could, for instance, enter 'one-year fixed-rate savings' or 'three-year fixed-rate mortgage', put in details such as how much you have to save or how much you want to borrow and what the property is worth and it will come up with a listing, showing all the relevant providers which you can then rank on highest/lowest interest first based on current rates.

What you cannot do is to buy directly from this site. There are no 'click-throughs'. But armed with the information you have gathered, you can then approach a high street outlet or a broker or go to the company direct by phone or email.

You have the reassurance that the listings do not ignore companies that do not want to be in tables because they are bad value for money or that object to paying for entry into commercial comparison sites because they do not regard this as money well spent from their point of view.

The particular disadvantage of the site is that it does not include many products such as car and home insurance, which are annual spending decisions. Nor does it cover longer term insurance policies such as life insurance. It is also biased towards the mainstream, so if you are looking for a mortgage and you know you have had credit repayment problems in the past, this site will not help you – you will have to consult a specialist broker. But that is probably true also of the vast majority of commercial sites, which are only intended for the mainstream purchaser.

Price-comparison sites are a great way to access a wide range of insurers – more than you could ever contact directly yourself. It is worth trying more than one comparison site though, as you will find that different insurers offer the best deals to different people.

 You can contact the Financial Services Authority via www.fsa.gov.uk or go to www.moneymadeclear.fsa.gov.uk, which is the FSA's own comparison site.

Staying loyal can be bad news

Saving money can demand effort. Many companies privately regard those who are not prepared to put this work in as 'apathetic' and not worthy of the best prices, which tend to be reserved for new customers.

It is common for companies, especially in areas such as credit cards and mortgages, where all the products provide much the same service (even though some will be better value for money than others), to regard bringing in new customers as more important than keeping those it already has. So if you see an advertised deal from your mobile phone company or your broadband supplier or your mortgage lender that appears to be better than your present arrangement, it is unlikely that you will be automatically placed on the more advantageous tariff. The same applies if you have savings. Attractive accounts are almost always aimed at prospective customers rather than those who have already signed up. However, while you will not automatically be upgraded to better deals, many companies will offer you something better if you threaten to leave.

Some mobile phone companies may have an option when you call them known as, 'Are your thinking of leaving us?' Others name this department 'customer retention'. Whatever the name of the department, almost all organisations will put you through to someone who is prepared to look again at what you are paying if you threaten to take your business elsewhere.

BE PREPARED TO DO YOUR RESEARCH

The route to saving money is to check competing deals regularly to see if you could do better elsewhere. Suppliers in all sorts of industries – from savings accounts to gas and electricity – know that a large slice of its customer base will not bother to look. They count on apathy.

66 While you will not be upgraded to a better deal, you may be offered an incentive if you threaten to leave. **99**

 Mobile phones and the myriad packages you can choose from are covered in full on pages 102-8.

Successful bargaining

To bargain successfully when taking business elsewhere:

- **Arm yourself with the information of what is around,** which you can glean from comparison sites. Don't hold back – it may be that some deals are not suitable or not available for you as an individual, but the person you are about to negotiate with does not necessarily know this.

- **Work on the 'I really don't care about you' attitude.** The people who work in these departments are trained to detect from your tone of voice just how serious you are about leaving, so never voice doubts such as, 'I really want to keep my email address' because this will be interpreted as a reason (or a weakness) on your part as many email addresses are dependent on staying with a particular internet service provider, so if you move, you need a new email, which can be a hassle.

- **If you do have reservations, keep very quiet about them.** The person on the other end of the line does not know what is important to you and what is not.

In most situations, the value-for-money seeker does not care who provides the service as long as it is good. Don't forget you can take your home and mobile phone numbers with you when you change companies.

Known value items versus unknown value items

It's all to do with what retailers call 'known value items'. There are some purchases where almost everyone can recite the price. Most people, even non-drivers, know the cost of a litre of unleaded petrol – it's displayed on a huge sign at the entrance to every filling station – and because it can be politically significant, any increase tends to attract media coverage. Drivers can be sensitive to a 1p-a-litre difference between one place and another nearby.

Likewise, regular supermarket shoppers know how much a loaf of sliced white bread or a litre of milk costs. Shops compete on these known value items –

however, they would not bother aggressively pricing Gorgonzola or Parma ham, for example.

A unit of electricity or a phone call is not a 'known value item'. Even where consumers have a vague idea of headline details, such as an interest rate or the cost of a call per minute, they have scant knowledge of all the other terms and conditions that can make up the whole pricing package. Suppliers are aware of this. They will often build in needless contract complexity to make it doubly difficult to compare offers but, when questioned, will say that customers are 'apathetic' about switching. This is a chicken and egg argument. Apathy may be caused by mind-numbing complexity.

The penalties of switching suppliers

The following is a brief resumé of the hurdles involved in switching suppliers as it's important to factor the financial drawbacks into the equation. There are more details on the penalties – and the opportunities – in the relevant chapters that follow in this book.

Banks and building societies

(For further information, see pages 30–8)

- **Loans** are notoriously difficult to move. Mortgages usually have minimum periods backed by penalties and exit fees.

- **Many personal loans** are for a fixed rate for a fixed period with extra interest charges for early repayment.

- **Credit cards** are easier to switch, but increasingly card companies that hope to attract you charge a percentage of your balance transfer. This reduces the value of the deal.

- **Savings accounts** are easier to switch, although you cannot move money invested at a fixed rate for a set period without a penalty or take money out of an account that requires notice such as 30, 60 or 90 days without paying the bank for the privilege.

Broadband

(For further information, see pages 114–15)

- **Most contracts** insist on a minimum 12 months – some go to 18 months. Suppliers say this is to pay for the supply of a modem as well as other set-up costs (including any introductory period of low charges). If you are likely to move, check you can move your connection with you and ask what will happen if your new home is not suitable for broadband.

- **One disadvantage of changing your supplier** is that you might have to abandon your email address if it is tied to your internet service provider – web-based services such as Hotmail, Googlemail or Yahoo get around this.

Mobile phones

(For further information, see pages 102–9)

- Unless you are on 'pay as you go', expect a 12- or 18-month contract period. Phone companies say this is to pay for the cost of the 'free' phone that comes with most new contracts. These rules are rigorously enforced. Moving home to an area where reception is bad/non-existent is not legally a reason for ending a contract early. Mobile phone companies say that mobile phones are not really for home use – they can be used anywhere.

- When your contract approaches its end, you generally have to give 30 days' notice – even if you wish to switch to another contract with the same phone company.

Gas and electricity

(For further information, see pages 12–22)

- Since both gas and electricity switching started in the mid-1990s, the rule has been that you can move whenever you wish, providing you give 28 days' notice. But now this rule has been scrapped. The rationale from regulator Ofgem is that this will allow companies to offer a greater range of fixed-term and longer-term contracts with better value.

- If you are held in a contract, you will not have to pay a fixed sum each month, as with a mobile or broadband contract, but you will also not be able to move elsewhere until you work through your notice period, so you are stuck!

You have to do be prepared to do your homework. Such suppliers know they don't have to worry about a large slice of their customer base, unlike supermarkets, which know you can make up your mind every time you shop – assuming, of course, you live in an area with supermarket choice.

Check any potential exit charges

Even where you have overcome the complexity or apathy (depending on which side you come from) of switching suppliers, there remains an even more significant hurdle – the costs involved in changing a contract (see the table on pages 26–7).

Present customers are often held in long-term contracts that prevent them going elsewhere without paying penalties, which can equal or more than outweigh the savings they could make through moving companies.

So before switching or asking your present supplier for a better deal by threatening to go elsewhere, look at your existing contract. You may find that you cannot leave until your contract term finishes, or that you have to pay a penalty to get out of your contract early, or that you are free to leave. The first and the third options do not present problems – you are either locked in or you can quit the deal at will. The second choice, however, needs some more care – and maybe some mathematics!

❝Check the terms of your existing contract before switching. You may be committed to a certain term or have to pay penalty fees.❞

Banking your money

What should you do if you are lucky enough to have some spare cash – even if it's just between payday and spend-day? Which investment options should you consider? This chapter delves into the world of investment and examines different types of accounts.

The current account

Unless you are willing to be part of the 'black economy' where everything is done for cash, living without a bank account is simply not an option for money savers (and that's anyone reading this book). This section looks at the choice of accounts on offer.

The vast majority of people now have a current account – that's a bank account that takes in money from you (and your employer) and lets you take it out again via cheques, direct debits, standing orders and from cash machines. Many people give little thought to their account with some people in their 60s still having the same bank branch name on their cheques as they did 40 or more years previously when they were students or in their first job. Such is the level of current account apathy that banks calculate the average customer is more likely to divorce than switch accounts.

But while all accounts from the big banks were once much the same – some even 'competed' on little more than how attractive their cheques looked – now that building societies and former building societies have entered the current account market, there are big differences between one bank and the next. Money savers are account switchers.

PLANNING A MOVE

When considering a move, work out which features mean most to you. These can include:

- **Access to a branch.** This can be important if you have lots of cheques to pay in or need special facilities. Disability access may also be important to you. But many customers never go near their branch – or any other.
- **Quality of call centres.** With more accounts now depending on the phone (and one major bank, First Direct, operating a phone-only system), the quality of a call centre is important. However, this can be hard to ascertain before you sign up, but you can at least ask where they are. If you prefer call centres based in the UK, don't be

> 66 Banks calculate that the average customer is more likely to divorce than switch accounts. 99

Money saving tip

You could run two accounts in parallel, if you are careful with managing each one, so you can see whether your new phone-based or internet-only account works to your satisfaction.

put off with evasive answers such as 'they are high quality'.

- **Whether you want an online account.** Most banks now offer online facilities to their customers, but these vary in scope and quality. You should get a higher rate of interest for an online-only account, but always check on access facilities if your computer is down – it's not money saving if you are severely disadvantaged or shut down completely when online access is blocked.

- **Interest paid when you are in credit.** Most banks pay nothing or a derisory 0.1 per cent (on which you have to pay tax) on what is on the credit side of your account. This interest will probably add up to no more than £15 a year at best on a typical account. Some of the newer current accounts do, however, offer more realistic interest rates, such as 3 per cent on balances in credit.

A more recent type of account pays a very high rate that is substantially over the current bank base rate, such as 8 or 10 per cent. These accounts usually come with strings – they require you to pay in a minimum amount each month (often £1,500–£2,000) so they automatically cut out the lower paid and most pensioners.

Banks usually also put a ceiling on the interest – for instance, it may only apply on balances between £100 and £2,500 and possibly only for a fixed period, such as six months or a year. But if you can fit in with their criteria without stretching

Money saving tip

If you have an interest-paying current account, try to arrange that direct debits come out of the account as late as possible after your monthly pay packet is banked.

your finances, and there are no obvious drawbacks, these accounts can make you a lot of money.

Beware of some accounts that charge you a fee if you fail to deposit £1,500 or £2,000 a month, so avoid them if your income levels vary from month to month. The banks don't average the good months against the lower paid ones – they just charge you for the poor-earning months.

- **Interest and other charges when you are overdrawn.** Saving money means staying in the black as far as possible. If you do have to borrow, always ensure that you arrange this with the bank ahead of your need to go into the red (for more on overdraft costs, see page 33).

- **Account-opening sweeteners.** You may be offered a gift to move your account – sometimes as much as £100. Always think about taking this unless there are strings to the offer, such as having to deposit a minimum amount either initially or every month, which you should avoid. Some accounts that offer a gift allow you to keep your old account as well so you can try it before plunging in.

Changing an account

Banks once took almost an eternity if you wanted to switch current accounts. This put many people off making a change. It should be easier now, though, so to get the best value from your move, follow these points:

1 Select your new account according to the features you most require, as outlined previously and answering the question, 'Will I be in credit or overdraft most of the time?' (see box, opposite).

2 Apply for your account, but don't forget that this will involve a new **credit check**. Current accounts allow you to go into the red, so banks insist on prospective customers passing a credit score test before getting their chequebooks and cash machine cards. They'll mark you down for debt problems, bankruptcy, not living long enough at one address, or even sometimes having the 'wrong' postcode. You may also be turned down if your rating has fallen (perhaps you have credit card or mortgage or loan arrears or have been in trouble with the courts), so never give up the old account until you are firmly established with the new one.

3 Set a date for the move. To avoid shocks and possible problems, make this as soon after your monthly salary is credited as possible.

4 Ask your new bank for the list of standing orders and direct debits it has obtained from the old bank. Go through them – you might find some money saving opportunities by striking out old magazine subscriptions or club memberships you no longer use or insurances that you have realised are poor value.

5 Your new bank will give you forms that you can give to your employer or pension provider so your payments go to the new account in future.

6 Be prepared for mistakes to happen. But under the Banking Code, to which virtually all banks subscribe, the bank you are leaving has to give your new account details of standing orders and direct debits within three days of receiving a request for a transfer.

Banks are not allowed to charge for closing an account and your new bank should have your account up and running within ten days. Banks have to refund any fees or penalties you are charged outside this period. Some banks also promise to give you cash compensation if a transfer falls outside the Banking Code minimum standards (see also page 205).

Jargon buster

Credit check Every time you apply to open an account where you can borrow (or be overdrawn), banks check up on your finances with one (or more) of three organisations – Callcredit, Equifax and Experian (see pages 56–9)

- **A free overdraft for students.** Banks often offer add-ons such as railcards to students. These are not nearly as important as the depth and length of the free overdraft that is nearly always a feature of these accounts. Students should also look at what will happen in the year or so after they graduate – how quickly do they have to pay back the overdraft?

GOING INTO THE RED

Most current accounts offer 'free' banking while in credit. Banks make their money when you move into the red.

Banks often publicise reductions on interest rates on authorised overdrafts – sometimes to as little as 8 per cent and occasionally for a 'special offer' all the way down to zero. But even at a more typical 15 per cent, it does not seem that expensive to slip a few hundred pounds into the red for a few days each month before payday. The banks also have rates for unauthorised overdrafts – when you go further into the red than you have agreed with the bank. Some say their unauthorised rates are the same as their authorised rates, although you will find that most banks do charge half as much to twice as much again.

Whether authorised or not, once you've worked out the interest, it might not sound too oppressive. But don't be deceived. The interest rate you see is just part of the story – and it could be a small percentage if you only occasionally use the overdraft or use it for no more than a few pounds at a time.

Money saving tip

The fee-free overdraft buffer is the amount you can go into the red without incurring any penalties, fees or interest. Depending on the bank, it can vary from nothing to £500, but most are between £100 and £250. It is intended to prevent expensive costs for those who drift a little into the red inadvertently. If you see your overdraft as a permanent extension to your spending power, there is a danger you will overshoot the safety zone and head straight into serious penalty area costs.

 For more information about how to handle debt, see the *Which? Essential Guide Managing your Debt.*

Look out for total borrowing costs

If the quoted APR (annual percentage rate) was the beginning and the end of the overdraft story, life would be simple, but banks make their real profits by charging fees for borrowing. In most cases, these costs are likely to far outweigh any interest rate calculation. Here are some of the most important factors to look out for:

- **Authorised arrangement/annual review (renewal) fee.** Some, but not all, banks charge you for agreeing an overdraft limit, even if you do not use it. Expect to pay 1 per cent of the amount with a minimum £10–£20 – and pay it all over again in a year's time. A few banks will only charge this if you arrange an overdraft over a certain limit, such as £5,000 or £10,000.

- **Authorised usage fee.** A few banks charge a fee whenever you use the overdraft. This is an alternative to the arrangement fee, not in addition to it. It is usually between £5 and £8 a month – or £60–£96 if you are overdrawn for at least one day a month throughout the year.

- **Unauthorised overdraft rate.** Usually around 25–30 per cent, but there will generally be an 'initial excess overdraft fee' of between £20 and £30.

- **Bounced cheque charges.** When you exceed your agreed overdraft, banks are entitled to refuse to pay cheques and direct debits. They charge anywhere between £20 and £39 for this each time something bounces, although some banks limit this to a set maximum each month. You could end up with a series of small cheques or direct debits bouncing because each one brings a charge that is larger than the amount of the cheque or debit. At the time of writing, there was a court case to determine the legality of overdraft penalty charges. However it turns out, the banks will try to find another way of raising revenue.

> ❝ Total borrowing costs might include renewal and usage fees, the unauthorised overdraft rate and charges for bounced cheques. ❞

Money saving tip

If there is no fee and you are creditworthy, it's worthwhile arranging an overdraft, even though you would not normally expect to need it. This sidesteps the 'unauthorised overdraft charge' if you go into the red. But avoid the temptation to spend it all – overdraft interest is expensive unless it is just a day or two and you will be worse off than you would otherwise have been.

BASIC BANK ACCOUNTS

All major high street banks offer 'basic' accounts to those who can't pass the credit test. These do not offer a chequebook. Instead, account-holders can have an unlimited number of direct debits so they can settle electricity, gas, council tax, phone and other regular payments. All accounts offer a cash machine card – some add in a debit card.

Deposits are made in the normal way by employers, benefits providers or by cash or cheque, but you cannot have an overdraft in a basic bank account. If you don't top up your account regularly or by enough, direct debits could bounce, taking you into the unauthorised overdraft charges arena.

PACKAGED ACCOUNTS

Banks are keen to emphasise 'free when in credit' current accounts, which have no direct charges. But they are also keen to sell 'packaged bank accounts' where the current account comes with a range of extras in return for a monthly fee of £6–£25 (or £72–£300 a year). Around one in five account holders have bought this add-on, often after receiving a sales call or sales letter from their bank.

The banks say these packages save customers money. It's horses for courses, but to check if they are good value for you, look at what's in the package, work out which features you would use, and whether you could obtain the same deals (or better) elsewhere. Always compare

Money saving tips

- Not having a bank account is costly. Many organisations charge more if you have to use cash. Energywatch estimates that the average user of pre-payment meters pays £173 more a year for gas and £113 extra for electricity – a total of nearly £300 (not counting the time and hassle of recharging the meter 'key').

- Most high street stores no longer accept cheques. Many other organisations now charge extra if you want to pay by cheque – or even settle by cash. These include most fixed-line phone companies, gas and electricity firms and even local councils charging parking fines.

- Phone companies typically add on £5 for each cheque that you send – where they accept them at all. That works out at £60 a year if you pay monthly, £20 if you pay quarterly. It is money wasted.

- But some phone companies also try to hide the charge – offering a discount for direct debit payments instead of a fee for a cheque. It works out the same – it's just better 'presentation'.

- Take care with joint bank accounts. You will be liable for its contents if your partner disappears – even if all the cheques were written by that person.

what's on offer with what you could get by your own effort outside of the package. Here are some of the headline points to be aware of:

- **Preferential overdraft rates and discounted loans.** You may get a 1 per cent cut from the bank's own rate, but you could find other lenders are cheaper still. Or you don't need a loan.
- **Discounted insurance.** To make sure this is genuine, it has to be applied after the quote is given as otherwise it could be built into the price. You will be limited to the bank's own insurance – you might well find cheaper elsewhere.
- **Discounted mortgages.** This is a competitive market so remember to look at overall costs and not just the headline rate. It is unlikely you'll make significant savings in return for a small monthly payment, but it could help.
- **Lower cost leisure.** There may be discounts on fitness clubs, but these organisations are always offering deals. You could do just as well, if not better, by asking the gym for a special deal.
- **Will writing.** This features in some of the higher cost packages, but you only need to write a will every so often and the cost of a solicitor is not expensive.
- **Motoring repair and roadside rescue.** The most valuable part of some packages. Check that it covers your own driving pattern (if you share a car, ensure it covers the other driver) and it includes 'at home' rescue if you would normally buy that.
- **Discounts on restaurants.** Like health clubs, you can probably arrange this

yourself. Many of the discounts are for less popular times such as Monday lunchtime rather than Saturday night – and you might have to pay a minimum amount, too.
- **Holiday discounts.** You might do better shopping around. In any case, most packages limit you to one tour operator so that's useless if you travel independently.
- **Shopping discounts.** Try best buys on the internet or a bit of haggling!
- **Commission-free currency and travellers' cheques.** Almost everyone offers commission-free currency because the profits are built into the price you pay for your euros, dollars, pesos and so on rather than on a percentage add-on. Travellers' cheques are poor value.
- **Travel insurance.** One of the more worthwhile parts of the package, but it may only cover the account holder and not a partner or family. There is some anecdotal evidence that insurers are tougher on terms and conditions when it comes to claiming. Ask about any medical conditions you may have.

If you consider a packaged account, calculate which features you will need or use. And if you buy, remember not to waste money by continuing with outside travel or road rescue cover.

❝ Discounted insurance must be applied after the quote is given. ❞

ONLINE BANKING

Online banks are authorised in the same way as high street establishments in the UK. They are also covered by the same financial compensation scheme if they go bust. This currently offers up to £35,000 per account holder in any one bank (or group of banks if they are owned by the same company).

Security and online banking

Security is a problem, with each new advance in countering fraudsters often quickly countered by identity theft and other scams. Up to £3.5 billion may be stolen each year in this way.

When faster payments start in May 2008, most banks will give their customers gadgets that will generate unique numbers only known to the account holders and their banks. But all the security in the world will not prevent fraud if you leave your computer on a secure account page at work while you go off for lunch!

Banks currently recompense most online fraud victims. But account holders can lose out if the bank decides they were careless or negligent or otherwise contributed to their loss. There is already a general presumption among banks that someone who loses money from a cash machine where the card and the PIN were both correctly used is in some way playing a part in their loss. It can be difficult to challenge this.

❝ Banks will give their customers gadgets to generate unique numbers known only to the account holders and their banks. ❞

The pros and cons of online banking

Pros
- Online accounts can save money because you don't need to travel to a bank branch.
- They often offer higher interest rates or other benefits.
- From May 2008, they should offer you virtually instant money movement so you can switch money from account to account or pay or receive money online.

Cons
- You will have problems accessing your account when the internet or your computer breaks down.
- Few online-only current accounts are so attractive that holders will want to give up access to the real people in a call centre or high street branch – the so-called 'clicks 'n' bricks' strategy.
- Security can be a problem.

Combine your current and online accounts

Most of us are not able to plan for our money with total certainty – even if you have substantial wealth, you cannot foresee the future. And some are just cautious people who want to stay in absolute control. So set up your banking by looking for an online current account that is linked to a high interest savings account. In that way you can move your money on a daily basis so you don't have to keep too much in a no or ultra-low interest current account.

❝ Look for an online current account linked to a high interest savings account so that you can move your money on a daily basis. ❞

Case Study Jessica

Jessica is a high earner with an after-tax salary of around £3,000 a month. But she has never thought about switching bank accounts – she still has the same account as she did when she was a student. She ends each month in credit of around £100 to £200. At the moment, her account earns 0.1 per cent interest, so she is lucky to pick up a few pounds a year. Moving to an online current account linked to a high interest savings account, she now looks once a week and switches money between the two according to her spending and saving needs. It's not too difficult as she only has two major outlays each month – her mortgage and her credit card. And once she gets into this routine, she finds it only takes her a few minutes. At 5 per cent, she manages to earn herself another £80 or so a year – enough for a good night out. Looking at her old account, she also realises she had been paying £8 a month for a packaged account, which she has never used. She cancels this, saving a further £96 a year – enough for a day away.

Beyond your daily needs

If you have some cash over at the end of the month, you need to find a home for it. There are literally tens of thousands of options, ranging from super-safe savings accounts to investments, which are little more than gambling.

SET UP A RAINY DAY ACCOUNT

The foundation of any savings plan is to start with depositing enough money into your 'rainy day' account. This way of saving is intended to meet the cost of any unforeseen problem, such as needing a new television set or putting right something at home that the insurance will not pay for.

The 'rainy day' account will save you money – lots of it. Getting small- to medium-sized loans – amounts up to £2,500 – is pricey. It can cost £500 (or 20 per cent) to borrow £2,500 over the course of a year through an unsecured loan from a major high street lender. If you have a poor or non-existent credit record, it could cost substantially more. But if you have some money ready, then you avoid having to borrow and the costs associated with loans.

Smaller amounts such as £200 can cost interest rates of up to 172 per cent if you have to resort to doorstep lenders because you are not creditworthy enough for a mainstream bank loan. And don't even think about unlicensed loan sharks.

Look for instant-access accounts

- Ensure that your money is in a totally safe environment. This is likely to be a savings account from a major bank or building society. There is no point in a rainy day account that can lose your money.
- Find an account that allows 'instant access'. This is often referred to as 'no notice' because it is likely the money may take a day or two to reach you. Ease of access is far more important than the rate of interest but these days most top value accounts allow quick withdrawals – with many offering the same interest rate on £1 as on £100,000 or more. You may find some savings accounts come with cash machine cards – useful if you need some money at very short notice.

Once an account covers these two rules, you need to find one that maximises the interest you receive.

❝A 'rainy day' account will save you money.❞

HOW TO SAVE FOR THAT RAINY DAY

Building up your savings so you don't need expensive borrowings for household emergencies is not rocket science. Instead getting that money together needs discipline. You cannot save and spend at the same time. You have to accept that if you are to build up a worthwhile cash cushion, you will have to make some sacrifices.

Saving means foregoing instant gratification. Don't make the big money wasting mistake of putting money away in a savings account while continuing to finance your previous level of expenditure on an ultra high interest credit card or costly high cost overdraft. Here are a few (almost) painless ways of saving if you are starting from scratch.

- Offer yourself a treat equivalent to the interest on your rainy account as your reward for a year of going without something you previously considered an essential.
- Put all the £1 and £2 coins in your purse or pocket at the end of the day in a piggy bank. Open this moneybox once a month and then bank the coins – banks have to accept these coins, but they can insist that smaller denomination coins are counted

and bagged up (they'll give you bags if you ask).

- Set up a regular direct debit from your current account so it goes straight to a savings account.
- It's usually sensible to try to pay off debts before saving because the interest rate you pay on what you owe is normally several times that of what you can earn on a deposit. But make an exception for low-cost student loans – you are forced to pay these on a regular schedule anyway once your earnings top £15,000 a year – because borrowing for an emergency will cost more.
- If you are giving up smoking (or any other expensive habit), encourage yourself by splitting the savings between your emergency bank account and building up cash for a big personal reward.

❝ You will have to make sacrifices to build up a worthwhile cash cushion. Pay off debts and give yourself a treat for going without something. ❞

For more information on savings accounts, see pages 41-6.

Moving beyond the rainy day

The first slice of savings is for a rainy day. The second slice is for a sunny day. This is money that you will not need to access instantly, so you can afford to do some long-term planning and be prepared to lose access to your cash for a while.

MAKE THE ISA YOUR FIRST STEP

The individual savings account – or ISA – should be the first destination for any longer-term savings. The ISA is a government scheme (although the state does not control the rates you get), which allows you to invest £3,000 a year into a tax-free savings scheme. This £3,000 annual limit rises to £3,600 from April 2008.

You should go for tax-freedom, even if you are not currently a taxpayer.

Money in an ISA carries on growing tax-free into the indefinite future. While you may now pay no tax, you may in the future be a taxpayer or even a top-rate taxpayer and ISA accounts are often among the best buys irrespective of their tax benefits.

❝ An ISA is the first destination for any longer-term savings because it grows free of tax. ❞

Compound interest

If you leave the interest to grow, **compound interest** works in your favour. Look at an ISA with £1,000 paying 5 per cent.

- After one year it's worth £1,050 in its tax-free home – compared to £1,040 for a basic-rate taxpayer in a taxable account and £1,030 for someone on the top rate, also in a taxable account. Doesn't sound much different?

- Now leave it for ten years and the ISA is worth £1,629, the basic rate account £1,480, while the higher-rate taxpayer is left with £1,344.

Someone saving the maximum £3,600 (£300 a month) over five years would build up £20,887 in an ISA, the basic rate payer would end up with £20,279 while the top-rate payer would have to make do with £19,686.

The ISA drawback is that once you take money out of your account, you cannot replace it. So it is intended for longer-term savings only. But most offer instant access when you want it – so this is not a reason to ignore it.

And if you don't like your ISA rate, you can generally move it to another bank or building society with a higher interest offering. To do this, ask the old ISA company to do this for you – you can't close the account and hope to move it somewhere else. A few accounts charge closure fees – avoid these as bad value unless they come with a guarantee of always beating a benchmark such as the Bank of England **base rate**.

> **"You can move your ISA to another provider, but don't close the account and hope to move it elsewhere: get it transferred."**

REGULAR SAVINGS ACCOUNTS

Many banks and building societies offer special rates if you agree to transfer a set sum each month by direct debit. You cannot usually vary this amount which, depending on the account, start at £10–£25 and could go up to £250 (a few have a weighty limit of £1,000 a month).

In return for the direct debit and accepting a number of conditions, you should be rewarded with a higher interest rate that will boost your savings over the year (and that's not counting the regular saving discipline, which will help as well!).

Conditions include:

- No withdrawals for a year.
- A limited number of withdrawals, but with a penalty.
- No interest at all unless you save for a minimum number of months.

You can compare ISA rates on a number of websites including Which? Money Best Buys at www.which.co.uk – click on the 'Money' shortcut. To access certain areas of the website you will need to subscribe to Which?.

Rebecca and Martin know they can only have one cash ISA a year each. They feel that between them they can put away nearly £7,200 – twice the individual annual limit from 6 April 2008 – although they will need to spend some of that on holidays. So Rebecca looks for a longer-term savings ISA where she gets a higher rate for tying up her money in an account that she cannot easily access. That also removes temptation. Martin accepts a lower interest rate in return for easy withdrawals, so they have ready money for late booking opportunities.

- Compulsory link to a current account at the same bank.
- Automatic switch to an account paying a poorer interest rate at the end of your contractual period.

With a few exceptions, most regular savings accounts allow you to access your money once a year, so they are a good way of saving up for an annual holiday or to save up a deposit on a home purchase.

Money saving tip

You may get more flexibility but not lose out on interest if you open a series of regular savings accounts at different banks in different months. Try this if you want to save for a winter holiday and a summer holiday.

"Regular savings accounts are a good way to save for an annual holiday or a deposit on a home. "

Other savings possibilities

The first rule of any savings account is to monitor its interest rate on a regular basis. Many banks come into the market with a mouth-watering record-beating interest level, drum up billions in business, and then let the rate slip back to a not very spectacular or even a totally humdrum return.

NOTICE ACCOUNTS

Where you have to notify the bank or building society a set number of days in advance when you want to make a withdrawal – usually 30, 60, 90, 120 or 180 – or lose the same number of days' worth of interest if you want your money back instantly, you should be offered a higher rate of interest than on an instant access account. Furthermore, the longer the notice period is, the more you should get.

This, however, is no longer always true. It is easy enough to find instant access accounts paying as much, if not more, than those with a notice period. There may be little point in tying up your money in this way. But banks must not offer accounts with strings, such as notice periods, which pay less than you could earn for the same amount in a no-strings account.

 Some accounts pay the same interest on £1 as on £100,000, but others are tiered so the higher your balance, the greater your interest rate. Always look at what you will earn – not what you might earn if you had more money. A number of tiered accounts pay less for £100,000 than some instant access accounts pay on £1.

FIXED-RATE BONDS

If you can afford to lock your money away for a fixed period – usually from six months to three years – you should earn more. And you will know how much interest you will get in advance. **Fixed-rate bonds** are a gamble. If interest rates go upwards, you might have been better off in a variable instant access account, but if they stay the same or go down, then the fixed rate works out more

❝ The longer the notice period for withdrawals, the higher the interest rate should be. ❞

(plus a smaller interest rate). These generally run for two, three or five years with no interest paid if you want your money back before one year and reduced rates before the full maturity date. Some National Savings products are tax-free. Money savers on the top tax rate should consider these but non-taxpayers should avoid them.

profitably. In theory, banks set fixed rates looking at indicators of interest rates over the next few years from the financial markets so they should be 'future-proofed', but nothing is for certain.

Long-term fixed-rate bonds are a good way of taking money out of temptation's reach, so even if you might lose marginally on the return, you will at least have your capital intact, which could save you money in the future when it comes to a major purchase.

Some bonds allow one withdrawal a year – or a withdrawal for which you pay a penalty, such as losing three months' worth of interest. But the more flexibility you get, the lower the rate will be.

National Savings & Investments (NS&I)

NS&I has a number of fixed-rate, fixed-term deals, including Savings Certificates with a stated interest rate and Savings Certificates tied to the rate of inflation

TRICKS OF THE SAVINGS ACCOUNT TRADE

Savings accounts in UK-approved banks and building societies come under the financial compensation scheme, so the first £35,000 is guaranteed if the bank goes bust. Other than reading terms and conditions, however, there is no guarantee that there will not be some small print, which takes the shine off the headline rate you are offered.

- **Start high, move lower.** Banks move into the market with a publicity grabbing rate. Then it becomes less attractive over time compared to rival deals. The bank counts on the apathy of savers not to move.
- **Introductory rates.** This is a promise to pay a high fixed rate or a substantial extra over the bank base rate, which is headlined but only lasts for a number of months (or until a set date).

To find out more about National Savings and Investments certificates, go to www.nsandi.com.

- **Bonus rates.** These are much the same as introductory rates – the small print may say that the advertised rate includes a percentage bonus for a number of months only. If you are disciplined enough to look again when the introductory or bonus rate ends, then these can be good money saving ideas.
- **Withdrawal fees.** You might have to pay to get your own money back, even if you want to close the account. These will generally, however, give you fee-free transfers of your interest.
- **The charity/good cause/sporting club link.** Accounts linked to a cause often pay lower interest with the promise that a 'contribution' will be made to the charity or club. You would usually do better aiming at higher interest and making a charitable donation through GiftAid, the government scheme that allows registered charities to reclaim income tax on your behalf. Big sporting clubs hardly need your extra pennies but some accounts offer 'goodies', such as shirts and piggy banks in club colours, which can be attractive to children (and some grown-up children as well) with smaller balances.
- **Branch-based accounts.** If you want the convenience of being able to access your account over the counter at a local branch, you will probably have to pay for this with a lower interest rate. Value-for-money hunters tend to aim at postal, phone and internet accounts.
- **Passbook accounts.** Most banks and building societies want to phase out old-fashioned passbooks. Some have done this by telling account holders they have to choose between the passbook and a more modern cash card access to their money – and if they keep the passbook, the interest rate will drop to a derisory level. Others have not even bothered to tell savers – they have quietly dropped the rate, relying on customer apathy.

❝Rather than take out an account that promises a contribution to a charity, go for higher interest and make a donation through GiftAid.❞

Beyond the savings account

This section involves taking risks with your money. You might gain more than from a savings account or you could lose a lot – even everything. If you cannot afford to lose any money, then this section is not for you. You would be better saving your money somewhere safer.

CONSIDER THE RISK/ REWARD EQUATION

Professional fund managers handling tens of millions every day know that behind all their computer screens and mathematically driven strategies lies a simple truth. The higher the reward you seek, the higher the risks you take of losing it.

It's easy to find out where risks start. Look at what you can get in interest on your savings on the best value savings account that ties up your money for a time – all the 'beyond savings' products in this section involve longer-term decisions, mostly measured in years rather than months or weeks. This is the 'risk-free' level.

Suppose the interest rate is 5 per cent. Anything below that is a missed opportunity, but anything that promises better than that will put your money at greater risk. There are degrees of risk ranging from not much more than the building society to the equivalent of backing an outsider at the racetrack. The further away from the risk-free zone you go, the greater the risk.

Advertisements and financial advisers are not allowed to promise high returns when selling **investment trusts**, **unit trusts** or **insurance bonds** – all ways of packaging up a portfolio of stock market investments for small savers. But they can certainly hint that you would do better than in a bank or building society account with what they are selling. If they are wrong, they will always point to the small print, which tells you that what you've bought can go down as well as up.

Jargon buster

Insurance bond A complex lump sum investment designed mainly for older people with larger sums of money. It can have some tax benefits

Investment trust A company whose only purpose is to invest in the shares of other companies so it is a way of buying a well-spread portfolio

Unit trust (also known as open-ended investment companies or OEICs) These offer a way into buying a basket of shares. Most limit their investment to one type of company either by geography, such as Europe, Japan, UK or US, or by business, such as technology or natural resources (mining, agriculture)

REDUCE RISK WITH A MONTHLY INVESTMENT SCHEME

Buying into an investment package in the wrong area or line of business is an obvious risk. The only people involved who did not lose their shirts in the 1999–2000 dotcom boom were the investment managers who sold packages of high tech internet shares to small investors on the promise of huge gains. The managers kept their salaries and bonuses; the investors saw their dreams of riches crumble to nothing.

If you invest in a package of mainstream shares through an investment or unit trust, investing on a bad day is a serious risk. You can reduce this risk, however, by joining a monthly savings scheme where you agree to pay in a set sum of money each month. When prices are high, your money buys fewer shares – when they are low, you get more for your contribution.

These schemes leave you in control. You can start, stop, restart, increase or decrease (down to the minimum) your monthly amount whenever you want without cost or penalty.

Most monthly investment plans start at £50, but some go as low as £20 or £25. You do not get any benefit

from putting a large sum with one scheme; indeed, it may be better to spread your money around and it does not cost any more.

LOOK FOR LOW COSTS

Whatever risk level you are happy with, you can improve the odds in your favour by aiming at the lowest cost product around or ensuring you cut a deal with the broker to rebate you some of the commission paid. Saving money means not paying for anything unnecessarily, and this applies to investment managers as much as anything else.

Packaged investments, like everything else, come with a cost. And the lower that cost – known as the Total Expense Ratio or TER – the better it is for you. Compare a fund with a TER of 3 per

You can get more details on investment schemes from the Association of Investment Companies at www.theaic.co.uk and IFA Promotion at www.unbiased.co.uk (see also page 209).

cent with one of 1 per cent which otherwise invest in the same shares. The manager of the first has either got to produce 2 per cent more a year every year (that's difficult) or you end up getting less. Over five to ten years, those percentage points add up to serious money.

Cost versus care – it's no contest

What do you get for your extra TER? Nothing. No one has ever shown any correlation between high costs and successful managers although managers after a good year might use their good performance to hike up their fees (you can bet they won't lower them after a poor year). Some top-performing funds have high TERs, others are well below average – there is no pattern.

You'll need to look for the TER – managers prefer to publicise the lower 'annual management charge', but even this can vary widely. For example, one fund that invests in all the mainstream shares in the UK stock market has a 1 per cent annual management fee, whereas another fund covering the same investment area in the same way is as low as 0.3 per cent – again, however, the extra does not benefit you at all.

Fees earned by sellers

Unit trust brokers earn a standard 3 per cent of your money upfront when they sell you the product plus 0.5 per cent a year 'trail commission' thereafter. Some probably earn their cut because they sit down with you, hold your hand, discuss all the possibilities and really know their stuff. Others just send you an application form in the post.

It's fine to pay for good value, but if the broker does little other than point you towards a list of names or even less, such as simply processing your purchase order, demand a commission rebate. Entering 'unit trust discount broker' into a search engine produces those who will give you money back. Some will rebate all of the money that you paid upfront

Money saving tip

If you bought unit trusts from a non-discount broker in the past and you are not receiving a value for money on-going advice service, you can transfer your holdings to a discount broker who will then rebate your trail commission. There is usually an annual fee for this – £35-£50 is typical - so this works best for those with larger portfolios.

 The Investment Management Association website has a TER comparison tool – go to www.investmentuk.org/investors/find_fund.

(the 3 per cent), while others will share the 0.5 per cent trail with you – or a mix 'n' match of the two commissions. Or, if you are happy that you know what you want, try a 'fund supermarket' – you go round, pick what you want and pay a lower price, just like in retail superstores.

 Never buy a unit trust directly from the fund management company. You will receive no advice and you will pay the same costs as going through a broker or funds supermarket but without getting a commission rebate. This is a no-brainer.

❝ Advisers and banks don't like investment trusts because they don't pay commission, but many have low costs and offer good value. ❞

WHY ADVISERS HATE INVESTMENT TRUSTS

Investment trusts are stock market vehicles that invest your money in shares of other companies to make the most of your funds. But they are one of the financial world's best-kept secrets. They will never be recommended by banks and it is rare for an independent financial adviser to suggest them.

Why? Advisers say they are complex, risky and not suitable for smaller investors, but the real reason is they do not pay commission. And because of this, many have low-cost or no-cost purchase plans coupled with annual management charges that can be more than a whole percentage point lower than a unit trust, giving better value for money that grows every year as you save more.

STOCK MARKET DEALING

Buying and selling individual shares on the stock market demands a lot of knowledge and skill. Unless you have at least £100,000 to 'spare', you'll probably find stockbrokers are not interested in giving you personal advice, so you are really on your own. The technical expression for no advice on shares to buy is 'execution only'.

 Investment trusts come in all shapes and sizes, but the most popular with small savers are the large trusts (mostly with assets worth over £550 million), known as 'global growth'. You can find more details on www.theaic.co.uk website.

Getting rid of unwanted shares

A large number of shareholders want to sell – perhaps odd parcels of shares acquired through a privatisation or a building society or insurance company demutualisation – or from an old employee scheme. If that's you, you have choices. You could:

- **Find the cheapest stockbroker around** as your only interest is in cashing in. This broker will probably offer a low-cost service if you send in the certificate by post and wait for the cheque. Stock market sophisticates will say that means you won't know the exact price you will get. That's true – it could be greater or less than the value on the day you decide to sell – but if you've held on for years, a few days will probably not make much difference. You may find some brokers will do this for a tenner or so.
- **Ask the company who sold the shares** if it has a dealing service. Holders with tiny amounts of shares are a nuisance to most companies because of the amount of costly paperwork they have to send out each year, so they might sell them for you for nothing or a cut rate.
- **Give the shares to charity.** This will not involve costs for you, which can be out of all proportion to their value if your holding is tiny. The charity will arrange tax relief for your donation.
- **Exchange your shares** for units in a unit trust. Many trust managers will do this for nothing. But they may not want esoteric shares in small companies. This is a way of staying in the stock market but without the hassle of many tiny stakes.

❝ If you only have a few shares in a company, a stockbroker might sell them for you for free or at a cut rate to avoid the nuisance of sending you paperwork. ❞

BUYING AND SELLING FOR THE MORE SERIOUS INVESTOR

Online execution-only stockbrokers do not just compete on price for investors who are going to deal several times a year (or even a month). They also rival each other on add-ons. If you are serious about dealing in stocks, you will need an account, which is like a bank account except the money going in comes from share sales and the money going out is for what you buy.

Here's a checklist of questions to ask before signing up – many stockbrokers offer a month or other period of free dealing, so you can try them out.

- **Account size.** What is the minimum deposit that I have to place to start with, what is the minimum after that, and how much interest do I get if my account is in credit?

51

- **Online accounts.** Find out what is available to you at the touch of a mouse. Will this be backed up by printed material?
- **Markets.** All brokers are able to buy UK-quoted shares, but ask if you need foreign stocks or UK shares on 'junior' markets, such as **Plus** and **Alternative Investment Market**.
- **Charges.** Are there upfront account set-up costs? Is there a minimum charge? Is there a monthly subscription fee whether you use the service or not that month? Is there an extra charge for tax certificates for your tax return?

CHOOSING A STOCKBROKER

Stick to stockbrokers who are online only or those who promise never to contact you with 'recommendations' by phone. Some 'best-buy' stockbrokers offer a bargain basement dealing service but then recoup their costs and more by pressure sales of high-risk UK and foreign small company shares, which you could find difficult if not impossible to sell. They may have a financial incentive to sell these shares, many of which end up virtually valueless.

These brokers will structure this selling so that you ultimately bear personal responsibility for taking their advice. It's not value for money saving a few pounds on a deal and then losing thousands by buying dodgy shares.

❝ Check out the charges. Are there upfront set-up costs or a monthly subscription for a service you don't need? ❞

 You can find a good listing of low-cost stockbrokers at www.ukcitymedia.co.uk/stockbrokers/idealing.

Borrowing for your lifestyle

You are what you owe. It's difficult to get through life without a loan. Students emerge from college with five-figure debts and we often buy almost everything else from our homes to our cars to the clothes on our backs on credit. You can easily spend half or more of your income on loan repayments. This chapter shows how to minimise what you pay.

Do you really need to borrow?

No one lends nothing for nothing – even if the interest rate in the advert is a big fat zero. Zero per cent always comes with catches – you might move into a hefty rate and never go back down again if you are even a day late with a repayment, or the price of those 'interest-free' goods might have been boosted to make up for the 'free' credit.

So every time you borrow, there is either a cost upfront or one that is hidden away out of sight. These costs vary greatly – from the reasonable to the absolutely exorbitant with interest rates not far short of 200 per cent a year (and we are not talking illegal loan sharks either). It is easy enough buying mainstream products from high street stores to pay nearly twice the price on the label once you factor in interest payments. At least two high street storecards – credit cards that you can only use in the chains of shops that issues them – have interest rates over 27 per cent. If you bought £1,000 worth of hi-fi and paid the debt back at the slowest rate the card lets you repay, you would end up spending around £2,000.

A lot of what we buy on credit is a waste because so many of us purchase on impulse or go shopping to cheer ourselves up when we are feeling low. We buy clothes we never or hardly ever

> **Some storecards have interest rates over 27 per cent.**

Before buying on credit, ask yourself ...

- Do I really need what I am about to buy?
- Could I wait until my next payday or put it off even longer?
- Have I worked out the affordability of this and its impact on other payments I have to make?
- Am I aware of all the terms of the deal including what would happen if I was even a day late in making a repayment?
- Am I borrowing more than I really need?
- Am I relying for the repayments on a pay increase/bonus/commission/overtime payment that may never come or which may not last for long?

wear. We buy music we never listen to. We buy cars that go beyond getting us in comfort and safety from A to B because they will impress our friends and neighbours. And then – this is worst of all – we sometimes buy more credit deals to pay off the credit deals that we can no longer afford. To help overcome stepping over this boundary, see the checklist of questions to ask yourself before you sign any credit agreement or use that card (see box opposite).

The best way of saving money is not to spend it and stick it instead in a high interest bank or building society account. The second best way is only to spend what you have – some people ration themselves by buying everything with cash from a bank account that does not allow overdrafts.

But few of us can avoid debt for larger items – and even fewer can afford to buy their first (or second or third) home with anything other than a mortgage. So debt, in one way or another, is a factor in most

❝ The best ways to save money are not to spend it or to ration it, but today debt is a factor in most people's lives. ❞

people's lives. If you can't be totally debt-free, then the next best thing to holding on to your cash is to ensure you get the best credit options around.

THE BEST-HEELED GET THE BEST DEALS

It's a fact of credit that the less you need a loan, the more eager the banks are to lend money to you and the lower the interest rate you will pay. But no matter how much you need it, you have no automatic right to credit. Lenders can and do turn down applications, generally without giving a reason.

They do not have to explain why you are not suitable. They work on the basis that the more anxious you are to borrow, the more likely you are to 'default' – pay late, get in arrears or not bother repaying the loan. They are only interested in your ability to repay – not appeals based on why you want a loan.

They will ask you about your earnings. Banks reckon someone earning £100,000 a year will be more likely to afford repayments than someone on £10,000. So your interest rates should be lower. Although they do not always check salary statements, remember that it is a criminal offence to knowingly lie about your income. Banks will probably check your earnings for a mortgage, rarely for a credit card.

For more information about high interest bank or building society accounts, see pages 30–52.

Your credit reference

Lenders generally make decisions based on your credit reference files. Every time you apply for a loan – whether a credit card, storecard, longer-term bank loan, hire purchase or other financing on a car, or a mortgage – the lender will run your personal details through a check with a credit reference agency.

There are three main credit reference agencies – Callcredit, Equifax and Experian – and although the details each has on you may vary a little, the overall impression that a future lender will get is likely to be similar whichever agency it deals with.

The agencies only supply information to lenders about you. They do not make decisions. It is up to each lender to make up its own mind how to interpret the information. Some lenders only want borrowers with pristine records; others, who generally charge more, are prepared to lend to those who may have had past problems with repayments.

Credit reference agencies start off with the electoral roll – the annual listing of who votes where. This establishes that you really exist and were, at least when the list was compiled, living at the address you give (the recently moved have to supply previous addresses).

If you fall at this hurdle, you will be almost certainly automatically turned down. You'll either have to go without or go to a fringe lender who will charge a very high rate.

Money saving tip

Checking your credit record on a regular basis will ensure there are no mistakes. Errors can often arise where you have a similar name to someone who lives in the same postcode as you or where you have had a dispute over goods or services. Pages 57–8 tell you how to find out what's on your file and how to get it rectified if it is wrong.

 To find out more about the main credit reference agencies, go to www.callcredit.co.uk, www.equifax.co.uk and www.experian.co.uk.

What your credit file tells you

There is a difference between what you see when you apply to view your file and what a financial company gets to know. The record you are given will show your credit limits and how much you actually have outstanding and with which lender or credit card company. But a bank will not get these details. What the record shares with you is whether the repayments were on time, late or missed altogether and whether you have had **county court judgements** (CCJs) listed against you in the past six years and if you have been judged bankrupt. It can see how many applications you may have made for credit, although it will not know any further details. You can buy a paper version of your file for £2 but there are several more expensive services if you wish to look at it regularly – see each company's website (opposite).

What your credit file tells a lender

Your file only has limited information about you. It doesn't:

- Reveal how much you earn or where you work.
- Mention your sexual orientation or religion or criminal record or the number of children in a household.
- **'Blacklist'** or **'redline'**. Some debt collectors threaten 'credit blacklisting', but they cannot do this because blacklisting does not exist – they mean they will try to put as many negative factors on your file to ensure you never get credit again.

Jargon buster

Blacklist A colloquial term for negative comments on your credit file, which could dissuade a lender from offering a loan. There is no official 'blacklist'.

County court judgements (CCJ) A legal decision against you that orders you to pay a debt. It may not be the amount the lender wants

Redline Where a whole area is seen by a lender as 'off-limits' rather than individuals living within it

66 Your credit file has limited information about you. It records how many applications you have made and sometimes has details of who has lived at your address. 99

- Show whether you were accepted for previous applications; nor does it say if you were turned down or if you were only accepted on more stringent than normal terms.
- Show if previous applications were for £15,000 or a £15 a month mobile phone contract.
- Say if your family or others living in your household are financially linked to you – unless they share loans such as mortgages or have an overdraft on a joint bank account with you.

But your credit file does:

- Record how many applications you have made for credit, but these have to be signed (or the phone equivalent where identity is asked for) applications that could result in your getting money – you are not penalised merely for asking a number of lenders for details of their loan products.
- Possibly have details of those who have lived at your address in the past six years, but there should be a clear distinction between former residents and those now at your home.

WHAT LENDERS WILL DO WITH YOUR REPORT

Lenders will look at your credit report plus information such as your salary that you will have to put on the application form and then activate one of the following options:

- Offer credit at the advertised rate – you should get this if you have a good record and can easily afford repayments.
- Offer credit at a higher rate – many loan adverts quote 'typical' interest rates – up to one-third of successful applications can be higher than this.
- Decline your application.

Strangely enough, lenders may not want borrowers who have never had credit before, even if they appear to be well off. They are suspicious of applications from those whose file is a blank. One reason is that they fear the applicant may not exist. But more importantly, they are looking for a past record of responsible borrowing and reliable repayments (including paying interest). A lack of record can especially affect those who are starting out in life – and those who are retired.

❝ Lenders are suspicious of applicants whose file is a blank as there is no record of responsible borrowing and reliable repayments, and it is possible the person might not even exist. ❞

IMPROVING YOUR RATING

Many applications are dealt with by computers, which simply look out for certain 'negatives'. No two lenders have the same criteria, but to prevent rejection or being accepted at a higher than advertised rate, you need to avoid:

- **Moving too often.** Ideally you should have lived at least three years at your present address. If you are a student or a young person who moves often, try to ensure banks and other lenders deal with you at a parent's address, which is likely to be more stable. Some lenders do not like borrowers who live in multi-occupancy houses.

- Telling them about any name change through marriage or other reasons. Lenders are suspicious if you appear under more than one name. This can be even more difficult for women who keep one name for work and another for home use. Warn them if there are other versions of your name, perhaps due to frequent mis-spellings.

❝Many applications are handled by computers that look out for 'negatives', such as moving often or living with multiple occupants. ❞

Case Studies   Janine and James

Janine applied for a £4,000 loan to buy a car. She stated her earnings as £19,000 a year and the bank believed that was enough to fund the repayments. It looked at her credit record, which shows she has lived at the same address for five years. The bank liked this. It also liked the fact that she had held a credit card for four years, which she had always settled in time each month. It believed she was responsible so she got the loan at the advertised rate.

James, however, also applied for a £4,000 loan to buy a car. He stated his earnings as £18,000. The bank looked at his credit record, which showed he had moved home five times in four years. This raised warning signals at the bank, so it went through past addresses and found he had changed his name a little from time to time – Jim, Jimmy and Jamesie. He had also had moderate arrears on a credit card as well as making formal applications for six loans in the past four months. While none of this meant he would not pay this loan, it was enough to make the bank wary. His application was rejected.

Credit cards

Credit cards are the most common form of borrowing. Between us, we own 70 million of them in the UK. They are convenient to use and offer flexibility in how you repay, but be careful how you use them.

There are several hundred variants on the market, so just how do you choose the one that's best value for your needs? And should you have several? A 2007 Which? Money survey found 251 different cards, but only gave 20 its 'best-buy' accolade.

CHOOSING A CARD

Credit cards make money for banks when you go beyond the interest-free area and start to pay interest – even if you don't intend to borrow on the card every month. So you have to be careful in how you choose a card.

There are so many confusing – even conflicting – factors in how card companies calculate interest, that you

---

Zero (or very low) interest rates

A year or so ago, 'rate tarts' – people who are prepared to work hard to switch their loans wherever and whenever they can find bargain interest levels – could move their loans between cards to find a series of 0 per cent interest rates. Some even managed to get such large credit limits and applied successfully for so many cards that they could borrow up to £30,000 interest free for months (if not longer) on end by moving their debts around their cards.

---

have to look at them under several different headings to find a good value card. There are also other areas, such as annual fees and the implications of cash withdrawals that are important to bear in mind when choosing a card.

Start with the interest rate

The rate on your card is largely related to how creditworthy the card provider thinks you are. At the time of writing, rates range from 7.9 per cent to 39.9 per cent a year, but if the bank does not rate you in the top two-thirds of successful applicants, you might have to pay more than the headline number in the adverts. Some cards feature a much lower rate such as 1.19 per cent. Don't be fooled. This is a monthly interest figure. And, thanks to the complications of compound interest, you can't even multiply that by 12 to get the answer. Cards must show the annual percentage rate (APR) in their literature.

There is no way of knowing what rate you will get on many cards until you apply. And if you apply too often, it will become obvious from your credit record that you have been disappointed a number of times – marking your rating lower for future applications. There is no obvious way around this.

Beware of balance transfer fees

It's hard to find as many 0 per cent interest deals now – even harder to find a credit card that wants to take your balance from another knowing you will try hard not to pay it a penny in interest. But while there are still some zero-rate arrangements, these now generally come with 'balance transfer fees'. You might now pay 3 per cent upfront on the amount you move to a new card so the card has to have a lower interest rate.

Cards often allow you to add this fee to your debt, so they can eventually earn more interest on it. Note, too, that balance transfer cards usually limit themselves to sums from previous cards. So new borrowings will be at a higher interest rate. However, some cards come with 'capped' transfer fees, so there is a maximum cost to move your account. This can be good value for those with larger debts to switch.

Find out the order of payments

Many card companies have an 'order of payment'. They split your debt into as many as four parts – balance transfer from goods, balance transfer from cash borrowings, new purchases of goods, new withdrawals of cash. Each one might have a different interest rate.

They then often allocate your repayments to the lowest interest level debt first, so while your payments reduce your zero or low-rate amounts, those parts with the higher interest levels just keep on growing.

Money saving tip

Keeping one card for balance transfers and a second one for new shopping is the safest way around this. You should never put new purchases or cash withdrawals on the low or no interest card.

❝ With balance transfer fees you might now pay 3 per cent upfront on the amount you move to a new card, so to make it worth doing, the card has to have a lower interest rate. ❞

Case Study Louise

Louise paid 17.9 per cent annual interest on her £2,000 debt – that's a £27.80-a-month finance charge. But she was lucky enough to complete a switch to another card with five months' free interest (many only have three months), saving her £139. She had to pay a 3 per cent transfer fee on her balance (£60), but her total gain was nevertheless £79.

However, her new card took all her payments against the 0 per cent balance transfer, while all her new payments were charged at the card's standard rate of 18.9 per cent and any cash withdrawals at the card's even higher rate for cash of 22.9 per cent.

So now she is, in fact, paying a higher rate than before. This could, if she does not make a high enough monthly payment, end up costing her as much if not more than before.

Annual fees

The banks tried to impose these in the early 1990s and it proved so unpopular that they had to drop the idea. However, some are trying to bring it back in via the back door with monthly fees of £2 (low enough for the tricksy banks to hope you don't notice) or 'low usage' fees of up to £35 if you don't use your card enough each year. Because the vast majority of cards are free, there is absolutely no point in using one that charges – it's money down the drain. Some monthly fee cards claim they offer lower interest rates. They rarely do. But if you pay off in full each month, that is of no concern to you anyway.

You might, however, have obtained a card with low usage fees in the past and no longer use it. If so, get rid of it as soon as you can get another. Cancel any card that charges a low usage fee – what could be the point of paying for something you don't use?

Cash withdrawals

It's always a money loser to use your credit card to withdraw cash. All cards impose an interest charge – often at a higher rate than for purchasing goods and services. In most cases, the interest-free period does not apply – some also add on a fixed cash withdrawal charge.

Some banks now stretch the word 'cash' much further. The card companies also define the credit card cheques that are often sent unsolicited to cardholders (see pages 66–7) as cash. Foreign currency and travellers' cheques are also seen as cash. Even further, the plastic providers will hit you with cash usage fees for spending at online casinos (which usually demand a credit card).

A few banks even treat the gift vouchers and tokens that many stores sell as cash, even though they can only be used to get goods and can't be turned back into money. If you are not sure about whether your card does charge for gift tokens – and it is usually buried in the small print so you'll have to look hard – use another way of paying.

❝ It's always a money loser to use your credit card to withdraw cash. This includes foreign currency and travellers' cheques. ❞

THE CREDIT CARD SAFETY NET

A great advantage of using a credit card – even if you don't really want or need to borrow – is that you get protection against dodgy firms under legislation known as Section 75 of the Consumer Credit Act, 1974.

The legal jargon is that the card provider is 'jointly and severally liable'. In plain English, this means that the card company (or other lender) cannot charge you (or has to refund you) for anything you have bought that has failed to materialise. So you would have a valid claim if there was misrepresentation (such as a watch sold as solid gold being solid plastic covered with gold paint) or breach of contract (the goods you ordered either did not arrive or were faulty) by the supplier. You must first try to claim against the supplier.

Generally, however, this rule clicks in when a company goes bust. Anyone, for instance, who had bought vouchers in Christmas club Farepak with their credit card ahead of it going bust in 2006 could have claimed on their card. This rule is often used when furniture companies collapse or mail order firms disappear.

Claiming under the Consumer Credit Act, 1974

To qualify for a claim under the Consumer Credit Act, the goods have to cost between £100 and £30,000. You can claim if you have just paid a deposit on an item worth between these limits. You can claim if there are a number of items that are needed to make a whole – such as a three-piece suite. But you cannot claim if you buy low-cost unrelated items from a supplier, even if the total bill tops £100. Following a court case in 2006, this rule covers items from non-UK suppliers when:

- A consumer uses a UK credit card to buy goods while abroad.
- A consumer orders goods from a foreign supplier while abroad for delivery into the UK.
- A consumer in the UK buys goods that are delivered to a UK address from overseas by telephone, mail order or over the internet.

- There is face-to-face pre-contract dealings with a foreign supplier temporarily in the UK, or with a UK agent of a foreign supplier, but the contract is not completed in the UK.

The banks have launched an appeal to the House of Lords against this decision.

It is not worth using a credit card to purchase holidays from UK travel agents to get this cover, however. Most add a surcharge of up to 4 per cent – that's £40 on a £500 per head package for two people. You already have protection in most cases).

You are not covered by Section 75 if you use a debit or charge or prepay card. But it does work for many other forms of credit that are expressly linked to the purchase of goods.

❝ Don't use a credit card at a UK travel agent just to get cover. ❞

Case Studies Martine and Joanne

Martine bought a new kitchen borrowing £4,000 from a credit company in a loan organised by the kitchen supplier. The kitchen company then went bust, but Martine had a Section 75 claim.

Her neighbour Joanne took out a personal loan from her bank and ordered the same kitchen from the same supplier. But she couldn't claim under Section 75 because there was no link between the loan and the purchase - as far as the bank was concerned, the £4,000 could have been used for anything.

TYPES OF CARD

Both Visa and Mastercard are owned by the same major banks and credit card companies. There is no discernible difference between the two either in what they do or in how they treat consumers. There is also no visible difference between the two in the number of retailers worldwide that have signed up to accept their cards. Virtually all UK merchants accept both interchangeably although there might be some differences in some overseas countries. So it's a matter of no concern to money savers which one you go with. Many banks issue both varieties – and the points that matter such as interest rates are down to the banks themselves.

However American Express cards are less accepted in the UK. Some retailers refuse them and others hit the cards with a percentage surcharge (legal provided you are warned).

> **❝ It is the interest rates and terms that matter on a card, not its colour or being 'upgraded'. ❞**

What about gold and all the other colours?

This is pure marketing. Gold, platinum, silver, green – it's the interest rates and other terms and conditions that you should pay attention to, not the colour. Some banks try to persuade you to use a higher credit limit – and higher usage,

they hope – by 'upgrading' you to platinum or gold. In fact, you can now move straight to platinum with a number of banks if you have a regular income of just £15,000 – less than two-thirds the national average salary.

But a few banks now offer 'black' cards. These come with services that most people will never want – or at least be able to afford – such as ordering expensive jewellery and having it delivered when you forget a birthday. One is aimed at people earning a minimum £200,000 a year.

Cards that offer 'points'

Many people sign up for cards that offer 'points' – usually towards cashback or shopping vouchers and occasionally goods, such as electronics. These typically pay 0.5p for each £1 on the card although retailers that offer credit cards with their own brand, such as John Lewis, Sainsbury's and Tesco, may pay 1p in the £1 for what you spend in their store. Don't confuse these and similar credit cards that are labelled with high street names with storecards, which can only be used in one retailer or group of shops.

By putting as much spending as possible on the card, money savers can reap an extra reward – and that's on top of any store loyalty card scheme. Using the Tesco credit card and the Tesco Clubcard (its loyalty scheme) in Tesco means you collect benefits twice over. You could still get extra benefits if you used the John Lewis card in Tesco along with the supermarket's loyalty card.

Charity cards

Other cardholders opt for charity cards where the good cause gets £5–£10 when you sign up and around 0.25p–0.5p of what you spend after that. Not all these cards (technically known as 'affinity cards') are for registered charities – some cards support political parties or universities or sports teams.

USING A CREDIT CARD EFFICIENTLY

All these choices are fine and help you get the most out of a card. But banks are not stupid. They need to earn money from you, not provide you with a free service. They hope you'll slip up in one costly way or another. So to avoid hassles, you need to know how to use your plastic property. Banks take your cards seriously. So should you. This section has details on how to use your card efficiently.

❝ Banks take your cards seriously. So should you. ❞

Pay more than the minimum payment

Cards have a minimum monthly repayment. This can be the higher of £5 or £10 and a percentage of the balance outstanding on the debt. These percentages have reduced over time – it used to be 5 per cent but now some are as low as 3 per cent.

Freebies for applying

Some banks market their cards by offering a 'free gift'. These have included a reasonable watch, camera or set of suitcases. Strangely enough, if you pass their credit tests and get the card, the gift comes with just one string – you use the card once. There is no need to spend heavily as there is no minimum spend. It's not hard to find a way of using the card for something less than a fiver – a local train ticket, for example.

All you then have to do is to remember to pay this first bill in time. You can then shred the card if you want.

A few plastic providers have stands at exhibitions, agricultural fairs and sports events. Here you get an instant gift - perhaps an item of luggage or a few bottles of wine - just for filling out a form. For money savers this is an opportunity that could be just too hard to resist.

 The www.fairinvestment.co.uk website offers comparisons of charity and other affinity cards, such as those linked to sports teams.

If you stick to repaying the minimum, it could take years to clear your debt – indeed, it would go on for decades (if not for ever) for those who carry on using the card. For example, if you paid back the minimum 3 per cent (or £3) a month on a £1,000 debt, it would take more than 14 years to clear the loan on a 15.9 per cent card.

The first payment would be £30 with each subsequent one slightly lower. But if you were to keep the payment at the same £30 as the first month, the debt would be cleared in under four years.

Credit card debt is never cheap. Paying it off as quickly as you can is always the best solution.

 Many cardholders have a direct debit to pay the minimum each month. If this was left in place in the example above, the cardholder would have taken the 14 years – and paid hundreds of pounds more in interest charges.

Pay off the debt in one go

Around half of all credit cardholders see their plastic as 'convenience' rather than a loan. They use it to buy goods online or over the phone or to pay stores or restaurants or car repair shops but always intend to pay the bill off in full each month.

To keep interest-free credit card borrowing alive, the whole bill has to be paid off on time and completely each month. Leave even one penny and this deal dies. This is really sneaky!

If anything carries over past the due date, the bank then charges interest on the amount outstanding and on the whole of the next month's purchases from the date each one is incurred. But even if you pay off the next bill entirely, you could still find yourself cut off from 'free credit' because you have interest outstanding from the day of the bill itself until the day you pay, which you will not know about until the following month, resulting in debt the next month. And so it can go on.

Remember that free credit only comes back when the bank sees you are down to zero again. The only way to get rid of this is to desist from using the card for a whole month (perhaps using another one) or to overpay the bill by enough to more than beat the interest payments. You will then get a credit balance the following month if you do this and move back into the 'interest-free' zone.

Avoid credit card cheques

These are sent out – nearly always unsolicited – by a large number of credit card companies. You are sent six to eight cheques, which you can make out to anyone you like – including yourself. Once they are completed and signed, they are just like cheques to the recipients. The banks say they are a convenient way to pay bills and debts. But they are a really bad idea. Here's why:

- There may be a 'handling fee' – typically 2.5–3 per cent.
- The cheques count as a cash withdrawal, so there may be a higher interest rate.
- They do not count for any interest-free period.
- Purchases with these cheques are outside the credit card safety net (see pages 62–3) so you lose your valuable Consumer Credit Act protection.
- Security is lax – they are easy to recognise in their envelopes, so they are simple to steal. Anyone can then sign them.

The best idea is to shred them and use them for your hamster's bedding.

Don't use payment protection insurance (PPI)

Never tick the box to agree to 'payment protection insurance' (sometimes called loan protection cover) or, as some credit card companies call you, sign up on the phone. The PPI extra sounds hardly anything – 'less than a couple of coffees a month' is one sales pitch – but that can add up to tidy sum over a year.

Understand how the 'free credit' works

This is usually advertised at 56 days (some offer slightly longer or shorter periods), but it's almost impossible to get this because the stated time is a 'maximum'. As each month progresses, your 'free credit' period goes down so that the last payment before the end of your month only qualifies for 25 days (that's 56 less 31 days). It will take about a week to send out your bill so it's now down to 18 days in which to pay. Cheques take up to four working days to clear so you need to get it into the bank that much earlier – even sooner if you rely on the post, so that cuts down the 'free credit' period still further.

Money saving tip

Most cards allow you to set up a direct debit from your current account so that the bill is paid off in full every month, whatever your balance. This avoids forgetting, statements getting lost in the post or the problems that could occur if you go away from home. Remember that the due date can change each month – watch out especially around public and bank holiday periods such as Christmas and the New Year. You can also set up a direct debit to pay the minimum – this ensures you are not hit with penalties for a late or missed payment (typically £12) and your credit record remains pristine.

For more information about payment protection insurance and why it is a total waste of money, go to pages 97-8.

DOORSTEP LENDING

Many people need to borrow relatively small sums for just a few months – perhaps for Christmas, unexpected car or home repairs, school uniforms or just to get away for a few days. Borrowing like this is easy if you are considered creditworthy and have a bank account. But millions, around one in six, fall outside of this – they become dependent on 'doorstep' lending from specialist companies who deliver cash to your home and then collect repayments weekly. These companies make no formal credit checks.

The disadvantage to taking a loan in this way is the huge annual interest rate. You might borrow £200 and have to pay back £20 a week for the next 15 weeks: a total of £300. That sounds like 50 per cent interest, which is bad enough, but because you are repaying it each week and the total loan is over such a short period, the real interest rate is around 170 per cent. Borrowing £500 over a year might typically cost you £825 including interest.

Many interest rates work out at over 170 per cent on a yearly basis. And just as you finish one loan, the agent will try to persuade you to take out another. You might even find you are taking out loans to pay off interest on other loans. Illegal loan sharks charge even more – and may threaten you if you fall behind with repayments.

The better alternative for most people is the Credit Union where interest rates are capped by law at 26.8 per cent, but many rates are lower – typically 12.9 per cent. There are no fees. You have to show the Credit Union you are a responsible person by saving for a time (it can be as low as £1 a week) and you have to continue to save as long as you are borrowing.

> **"Around one in six people become dependent on 'doorstep' lenders who make no formal credit checks and charge huge interest. "**

 You can find out about credit unions in your area via local money advice centres, libraries and from www.abcul.org – the website for the Association of British Credit Unions (see also page 203).

Secured loans

Credit deals advertised on daytime television and in some newspapers often stress the word 'secured'. But don't be fooled. The security is on the side of the lender, not you. It means you could lose your home (or other assets) if you don't keep up the payments. The most common form of 'secured' loan is the mortgage you take out to buy a home.

APPLYING FOR A MORTGAGE

Mortgage basics are easy, but working out the essential points before applying will help find the best value loan for your home buying – there are thousands of mortgages to choose from.

- **Lenders look at your earnings** – and those of your partner if you have one. They will then multiply these figures to tell you the maximum loan they are prepared to give.
- **Lenders have a 'maximum loan to value'** or LTV. This jargon means that they will only finance part of the price of the property. An 85 per cent LTV on a £100,000 property equals lending up to £85,000. The gap between that and the sale price is the 'deposit' that you will have to find from savings or some other source such as your family. Some lenders will offer 100 per cent LTVs so you can borrow the lot, but this will normally cost a higher interest rate.
- **Lenders will value the property** to see if it is worth the price you intend

paying. This is to protect them, not you, for if you fail to keep up the payments, the mortgage bank or building society will take back your home – known as repossession – and then sell it to cover the loan you did not pay.

- **Your repayments will be spread** over a number of years – typically 25. The shorter the time period, the higher the monthly payments but the lower the overall interest charges, so you will pay less over the mortgage's life. Some lenders offer thirty-, forty- or even fifty-year loans.

Here are some frequently asked questions.

How will a lender know how much I (and my partner) earn?

They will usually want proof of your earnings from your employer(s). They will take into account bonuses, commission and overtime if they are regular and reliable. They will assess what they are prepared to pay on what you are currently earning so you do not have to tell them if you are likely to stop work or downsize – perhaps to have a family – over the next year or so. But you should consider whether you could still afford a home loan after such a salary cut.

What is the most I can borrow on my present salary?

This varies but a typical lender will calculate your maximum on the higher of 3.25 times your salary plus one times that of the lower-paid partner (if there is one) or 2.75 times your joint income. You can find higher multiples, but these may involve higher interest rates. Some lenders will offer higher figures to younger people – often professionals such as doctors or lawyers – whose job promises substantial salary increases each year.

What is the biggest loan that I can get?

Most standard mortgages go up to 90 per cent of the value the lender's surveyor puts on the property – so you need a 10 per cent deposit. The valuation may be less than you are prepared to pay – it should be based on what the lender thinks it could get if it sold the property. Beyond 90 per cent, some mortgage providers charge either a higher interest rate or a 'high lending charge', a one-off fee to reflect the higher risk the lender is taking because it knows that if it had to take your property back because you had failed with repayments, it might not get as much when that company sold it as it had lent you.

A few lenders are prepared to lend more than 100 per cent. They set up special loans, which can go up to 125 per cent – or one and a quarter times the property's value.

Why should anyone want to borrow more than 100 per cent?

Loans are based on the value of the property, not your total cost of buying a home, which could include legal fees, removal costs, survey fees and stamp duty. So you always need to factor these in to your calculations.

I work for myself. How does this affect my mortgage?

Lenders will normally ask for three years' worth of audited accounts. But if you cannot produce these – perhaps you have not been self-employed for long or you have an unusual source of income such as share trading – you can opt for a 'self-certification' or 'self-cert' mortgage. Here, you merely state your income and that you are satisfied that you can repay each month. It is up to the lender whether to accept this or not. Expect to pay higher interest rates for a self-certification loan.

Money saving tip

If you are thinking about giving up employment, it's better to apply for a loan while you are still in work than wait until you become self-employed.

Will I have to go through a credit check?

Yes. Lenders work on the basis that if you have messed up one loan, you are more likely to fail on another one. But if you have negatives, such as missed payments, county court judgements or a past bankruptcy, don't give up if you want to buy. There are a number of lenders who specialise in loans to those with previous problems. These are known as 'sub-prime' mortgages. Some companies only lend to those with just one or two black marks – known as 'near-prime' – while others specialise in those with severe defaults and judgements – these are called 'sub-sub-prime'. The more sub-prime you are, the more you will pay in interest. In some cases, you might be better off renting.

❝ Lenders believe that if you messed up one loan, you are likely to fail again, but some specialise in 'sub-prime' loans. ❞

INTEREST RATES ARE NOT ALL WHAT THEY SEEM

Lenders are obliged to publicise the annual percentage rate (APR) on their mortgage loans. And most compete with each other by trying to come up with the lowest rate they can. Having a low rate means publicity in best-buy tables.

But increasingly, the APR has become less useful as a comparison tool. Banks and building societies now add in other costs. These are usually the same whether the mortgage is big or small. These can include:

- **Legal fee.** To pay for the solicitor the lender uses as well as checks to protect you – typically up to £1,000.
- **Valuation fee.** Pays for the survey that ensures your property is worth what you say it is – typically up to £600.

Money saving tip

If you are 'near-prime', try high street lenders before sub-prime specialists. Finding a sub-prime loan can be pricey as mortgage brokers may add up fees of up to £2,000. Always ask them for a fee estimate before starting and whether they will rebate any commission they get from the lender – the jargon for this is 'procuration fee'. Watch out also for brokers trying to sell expensive and largely useless payment protection insurance (see page 67).

For more information about credit checks, see pages 56-9.

- **Application fee.** This is just a way of boosting the cost of the loan – typically up to £2,000.
- **Reservation fee.** Another way of getting more money out of you – typically £250–£400.
- **Exit fee.** You pay this when the loan ends or you move to another lender – typically £250.

You might not have to pay all of these fees. In some cases, lenders offer one mortgage 'fee-free' and another with fees. The first will have a higher interest rate to compensate.

Fixed fees benefit those taking out larger mortgages. So money savers need to make a comparison based on all their costs. Some lenders are moving towards a 'warts and all' version of how much a loan will cost in total by including everything and then working this out over two to five years. But there is no agreement yet on a standard method across all home loans.

> **❝** Fixed fees benefit those taking out larger mortgages, but there is no agreement on a standard method of showing loan costs. **❞**

THE FIXED VERSUS VARIABLE RATE CHOICE

When you take out a mortgage, you are taking a gamble on interest rates decades into the future – and not even the cleverest City of London economist can see that far away.

Fixed-rate mortgages

Here the interest stays the same during the life of the loan, which can give you security that your payments will not rise. You profit if rates go up, but if rates fall, you will lose out compared to someone with a non-fixed-rate (or variable) loan. Most fixed rates are for two to three years, but some go to ten or even 25 years.

Money saving tip

Try to avoid estate agents if you are selling your home. Putting 'sell your own home' into a search engine produces lots of websites where you can advertise your property for around £130. A typical estate agent charges 2 per cent or £4,000 on a £200,000 property. Going online and seeing what agents expect for a property like yours gives you a target price.

 For more information about different types of mortgage and their implications, see the *Which? Essential Guide Buy, Sell and Move House.*

Variable rate mortgages

With these mortgages– and that includes **tracker loans** and **discount mortgages** – you take a chance that next month's payments will be higher (causing affordability problems) or lower (which means you can relax).

Which type of mortgage works out better? It is probably horses for courses. If you are on a fixed budget because you are pushing at your affordability limits, then the fixed rate gives a lot of comfort and security.

Jargon buster

Discount mortgage Where the rate is promised to be a set percentage below the lender's standard rate for a fixed period

Fixed-rate mortgage A loan where the rate does not change for a set period – expect to pay a penalty if you wish to end it early

Tracker loan The rate automatically falls and rises in tandem with the official Bank of England interest rate

Variable rate mortgage The rate falls and rises according to the lender's own interest levels

❝ In the 1990s many people with fixed-rate mortgages lost out when the interest rate fell. **❞**

IT IS OFTEN COSTLY TO GET OUT

Back in the 1990s, many people took out fixed-rate mortgages to protect themselves against higher rates. But interest levels fell, in some cases very steeply, which meant that fixed-rate borrowers were often paying huge amounts more than those with variable rates. But such borrowers could not change because they were held in by huge fees known as 'early redemption charges'. In many cases, these were equal to, or greater than, the saving that could be made by moving to a lower cost loan. And borrowers had to find the money when they exited the mortgage – not always easy.

The mortgage company argument for early redemption charges is that if they let you escape penalty free, you would have a one-way winning bet so you could stay in the fixed rate when it suited and escape when that made sense. There are also penalties for leaving discount loans where you are promised a lower rate for a number of months or years.

Most penalties now last the minimum contract length on the loan, but they often reduce the nearer the borrower is to the end of the mortgage deal. For instance, a five-year fixed-rate mortgage may have a penalty of 5 per cent of the loan in the first year, 4 per cent in the second, and so on.

It is rarer now to find a penalty that continues beyond the mortgage contract – known as an 'overhang period' – but they do exist. Avoid these as they allow the lender to hold on to you on its own terms.

You can often transfer the mortgage, so if you move home, you take the loan with you instead of cancelling it and paying. But if you think you might give up on home loans altogether – you are moving abroad, say, or moving in with someone else – then look for mortgages without exit fees.

HOW TO CUT YOUR MORTGAGE COSTS

There are a few ways that a money saver can reduce the cost of a mortgage:

- **Get as big a deposit as you can.** The lower the loan as a percentage of the property's value, the better for you. You'll avoid high lending charges and you might get a lower rate.
- **Shun payment protection insurance –** it's expensive for what it is.
- **Go for interest-only loans.** Because you only pay the interest and do not pay off the amount you borrowed,

these are cheaper than repayment loans (where you both pay interest and chip away at the debt). But when you come to move you'll have to pay back the whole loan so you will either have to find the money from investments and savings or sell the property. The sale option could be tricky if property prices fall as you will have to find the difference between the sale price and what the original loan was. This is known as 'negative equity'.

- **Opt for daily interest calculations,** which are better than annual recalculations – as long as the interest rate is the same.
- **Cut monthly costs on a repayment** loan by increasing the mortgage's life. But the more you do this, the less effect you'll see. As the table below shows, the reduction per month becomes very small once you go past the traditional 25 years, but you could end up paying hundreds of

The cost of paying back a £200,000 loan at 7 per cent		
Length of loan	Monthly repayment	Total repayment
15 years	£1,787 a month	£321,660
20 years	£1,541 a month	£369,840
25 years	£1,405 a month	£421,500
30 years	£1,322 a month	£475,920
35 years	£1,270 a month	£533,400
40 years	£1,235 a month	£592,800
45 years	£1,212 a month	£654,480
50 years	£1,196 a month	£717,600

thousands more if you opt for a very long-term mortgage.

- **Check your loan allows you** to make overpayments, such as an occasional lump sum or a regular increase in your monthly payments. Doing either of these has much the same effect as opting for a lower repayment period in the first place. Most lenders now have this flexibility.
- **Avoid flexible mortgages** where you can cut payments or take 'holidays' from the monthly amount. Whenever you reduce the payment or take a month or two off, your debt mounts. You'll have to pay it back eventually – and it will cost more. It is the opposite of overpayments.
- **Use an offset mortgage,** which combines loans with savings or bank accounts. The amount in your account reduces the loan (until you spend it or withdraw it) so you pay less interest overall. And the 'interest' you get on your savings is not taxed because your spare cash is cutting back on your mortgage. That's the theory. But offset mortgages may have higher interest rates – and they are only really effective if you have lots of cash in your account. For instance, they benefit someone who is self-employed, may have substantial amounts of income tax and VAT in their account, which can be used until it has to be handed over to cut the interest bill. For someone on a typical monthly salary starting at £1,800 and going down to £50 by the end of the month, there is very little interest to earn.

REMORTGAGING

Swapping one loan for another has become very popular – encouraged by brokers who receive fees for this. It can and often does result in lower costs as many lenders put you on 'standard variable rates', which can be expensive once your fixed rate or other special deal ends. So it makes sense to look for a new lender.

But always try your existing mortgage firm first. Threatening to go elsewhere could result in a better offer.

Consolidation loans

Remortgage brokers often suggest you 'consolidate' your credit card and other loans into the mortgage, aiming for a higher amount this time around. They point out that the interest rate on a credit card can be as much as four times as high as a mortgage, and, because of rising house prices, you can borrow more now anyway.

It sounds tempting. But these loans are probably for short-term requirements rather than the 20 or 25 years of a typical home loan because they are taken out to pay for something that would need replacing every few years. Once the credit card loans are on your mortgage, you will be paying for them for a very long time. For instance, if you replace your car every four years, you should aim to pay off a car loan in four years – not 14 or 24 years.

You can, however, work out your repayments so that you benefit from this by discussing with the lender how you can repay the extra you have borrowed and the publicity will say 'tenants cannot apply'. What happens is that you have two loans with two interest rates, the second mortgage being more expensive than the first.

They work when you have 'equity' in your home – the amount your home would fetch over and above your existing mortgage loan. This can, if you stick to your plans, be a cheaper way of paying for a major home improvement than taking out an unsecured loan.

But your home is at risk – twice over. Both the first and second mortgage lenders can pull the plug if you default. The second mortgage company is more likely to do this. If you fail to keep up payments on an unsecured loan, you can lose your home.

over a short period. So what you borrow for your car will subsequently be paid back in a few years.

Another temptation with a consolidation loan is that you use the remortgage money to pay off your credit card loans – and then you max your cards all over again. This is not money saving, it's a route to ruin!

SECOND MORTGAGES

Don't confuse this with remortgaging where you swap one loan for another. Here, you take on a second loan – they are often advertised as 'secured loans'

❝ With a second mortgage your home is at risk twice over, because both lenders can pull the plug if you default. ❞

For more information on handling debt, see the *Which? Essential Guide Managing your Debt*.

Insurance cover

Insurance is often sold to give you 'peace of mind'. But that can come at a heavy price. And much of what insurers try to get you to buy is unnecessary – sometimes a real waste of money. You can save by understanding the real risks that need cover from those that just profit insurers. This chapter sorts out policy essentials from waste-of-time plans.

To cover or not to cover

You can buy insurance to cover yourself against almost any conceivable risk. But totally comprehensive policies that pay out on any eventuality you can think of – and some you can't even imagine – cost a fortune. You could hand over much of your pay packet to insurance companies or you could put the basics of 'risk assessment' into practice.

THE RE-INSURANCE GAME

Here's a secret insurance companies would rather you did not know about. Companies in the insurance world routinely insure themselves against having to pay out too much to policyholders by going to other companies called re-insurers. Some re-insurance plans kick in when claims across all the policyholders top a pre-agreed level. Others pay out a percentage of all claims. There's a whole range of possibilities, some very complex. Re-insurers often re-insure themselves with other re-insurers, leading to a whole chain of policies.

The importance of all this activity for consumers is that the rates that re-insurance companies charge insurance companies for the extra cover they want are negotiated between professionals, who all have a very good idea of the real risks of something going wrong. And although there are headline events every so often, such as floods, fires, ships going down, planes going up in flames, insurers know they only happen very rarely and even less often all at once.

Re-insurers don't look at what consumers pay for policies. Rather they look at what insurers pay out on claims. 'Fair value' policies, such as those from motor insurers, pay out most of the premiums they take in from policy purchasers to those with claims. Of course, they also have administration costs and commission to brokers to pay for as well.

But with over-priced and unnecessary cover, such as mobile phone insurance or payment protection insurance, the insurers only pay out a small fraction of what they take in (little more than 20–25 per cent with payment protection policies), the rest is pure profit. This is reflected in the rates re-insurers charge. Take, for example, travel insurance costs.

Holiday insurance and re-insurance

Travel insurance for two adults and two children spending two weeks in Europe can cost anything from around £20 to over £150. Both policies cover the same ground. But whether your insurer gives you the bargain basement rate or stings you for the maximum, the policy will be re-insured at the same rate. And that is around £3 per trip per person for this form of cover. The £20 policy gives its issuer a small profit after costs such as administration and marketing. The £150 policy has identical administration, re-insurance and marketing costs, but here the seller makes a packet in profit.

The most expensive travel policies usually come from travel companies or travel agents who sell a plan at the same time as a holiday. They will tell you that being insured is a legal must. However, while a policy is often desirable, it's not essential if you are travelling independently by buying your travel and accommodation separately. European Union package tour rules say the tour operator is responsible if you fall ill or die, so holiday companies can contractually insist on the cover so that an insurer will pick up the cost of medical emergencies instead of the holiday company. But they cannot insist on you buying their cover – you can choose from the market.

Money saving tip

If you take more than two holidays a year, annual travel cover is usually better value than buying a series of policies. But check you buy the right policy for your needs. You may need a more expensive policy if your holidays include winter sports or visits to the United States.

Ask the expert

Can I afford the loss? How can risk assessment cut my insurance bills?

There are two main types of insurance claim:
- Those where you can bear the loss yourself from your savings
- The catastrophes where paying for the damages or problem yourself would literally ruin you.

Claims in the first category might include a small burglary with just a few low-cost (and maybe out-of-date) electronic items stolen or minor damage to your car.

Those in the second category might include the total loss of the contents of your home in a fire or flood or causing a major car accident involving millions of pounds in compensation payments to the victims.

Risk assessment means you look at where your pain threshold falls between the minor event, which you can afford, and the catastrophe, which will ruin you. This will be different for everyone. For instance, if someone stole your car, you would probably be in financial trouble, whereas if someone stole your mobile phone, you might not be too worried – you could replace it with a low-cost model until your next contract is due or use that old, but still serviceable, phone that is lying unused in a drawer at home.

COPING WITH RISK

When you have decided what sort of losses you can afford to bear yourself, try to tailor a policy to your needs.

One variable component is the 'excess' – that's the first slice of a claim that you have to pay for yourself. On a typical home or motor policy, this can be anything from £50 to £1,000. An excess of £100 would mean the insurer giving you £200 after a £300 claim while a £250 excess would give you £50 from the same claim. Aiming at a larger excess has two money saving features:

- **The greater the excess, the lower the premium.** All policies vary, but as a general rule, agreeing to raise the excess from £100 to £200 will save around £35 to £40 a year. Savings increase the more you raise the excess but not necessarily in proportion because insurers know that you are more likely to make small claims than big claims. They – and you – gain more if you do not claim for a series of small items.

- **A big excess means you cannot claim** for items you might otherwise have asked the insurer to pay. This means that you retain your no-claims discount on motor insurance (and sometimes on household insurance, too). Then, because you are claim free, your next year's premium (whether it is with the same insurer or another one) will not be increased to take your claim into account.

SELF-INSURANCE IS A BIG MONEY SAVER

A variation on the money saving possibilities with the excess is not to bother with insurance at all. The theory is simple and explained in the case study, below.

Case Study   Azeem

Azeem had two bikes (one for weekdays and a sportier one for weekends and each costing £700 new), for which he would have had to pay two sets of bike cover charges on a policy. He had insured them against theft outside his premises as part of his home buildings and contents cover with each bike costing £25 on top of his £600 policy, making £650.

Then he shopped around for property and contents lower cost cover and found it for £380 three years ago. But this insurer wanted £110 each for the bikes. Azeem decided to self-insure – to take the risk of losing a bike on his own bank account. Each year (assuming rates stayed the same), he saved £270 (£650 less £380) – £810 in three years. Bikes are not replaced on a new for old basis on many policies so, had he claimed, Azeem would not have got the full cost of an equivalent bike. Now, he's saved enough to buy a new bike and, if he suffers a theft, his premium will not increase because he has had a claim.

Azeem took a calculated gamble on the bikes – he had always used strong locks and made his bike unattractive to thieves by removing the saddle when parked – and he is now so far ahead of the game that he can bank the bike money.

Haggle for all you're worth

When you buy insurance, especially motor or home and contents, either on the phone or face-to-face, it is very likely you will be asked what your renewal quote is and what is the best quote you have had so far. They rely on your honesty in giving answers.

Insurance companies ask this because they know that buying insurance is almost entirely driven by price. Therefore, if your lowest quote so far is £500, there would be little point in offering a policy at £750. The easiest way to haggle is to tell them what they have to beat – and if it is your present insurer's renewal – they will have to beat it by more than a few pennies as you will tell them that you are satisfied with the service you have had.

Not all insurers will want to haggle, however. The £750 quoted above might be intended to drive that particular customer away as it is someone with a risk profile the insurer would rather do without. For instance, some home insurers may only be interested in very large homes, not flats, or car insurers might specialise in sports cars so your underpowered mini is not on their radar.

> ❝ All insurers bear in mind the two costs of retaining and acquiring customers. ❞

TAKING A SECOND LOOK

But many will say they will have a 'second look' and try to find something they could change without really affecting you. For instance, on a home and contents policy, the insurer might offer to strike out a clause that offers you freezer cover or allows you to claim if your garden plants are stolen – you may not even have a freezer or a garden, let alone care. On motor insurance, it could be 'a reduction because you don't drive to work'. It's virtually impossible to know what these are really worth as policies are rarely broken down into their constituent parts and there are so many components used in calculating the premium. But whatever it is, it gives the insurer a way of bringing down the premium while only changing items that are of little or no importance to you.

Threatening to go elsewhere can be very effective with your present insurer. All insurers have two costs in mind although these are two sides of the same coin – that of 'retention' and that of 'acquisition'. Outside a few specialists, such as those that cover works of art, insurance works on economies of scale. If they fail to retain you, they need to replace you with an 'acquisition' (insurance jargon for new customer), and for a typical company and average customer, that costs £50–£60. At least some of that should be yours as your reward for staying.

WARNING: DON'T UNDER-INSURE

Before looking at some specific ways you can legitimately cut your insurance bills, one thing not to do is to understate the value of what you want to cover. If your car is worth £5,000, don't say it is valued at £2,500. A £2,500 car value will cut the premium by a few pounds compared with what you would pay for the real £5,000, but when it comes to claiming, you'll be hit by a little known but legal insurance trick called 'averaging'. Suppose your car is stolen. You know you can't claim for £5,000 because you said it was worth £2,500. But you won't get the £2,500 either. Because you only paid for half the car, the insurer will cut your claim by half as well so the most you will get is £1,250 – half the insured value but a quarter of its replacement cost.

If you do not know the present price of your car, tell the insurer that you want to cover it at 'market value'. Those with cars that are worth substantially more than the market value for the same vehicle of the same age – particularly low-mileage vehicles or classic cars, for instance – should negotiate an 'agreed value' or 'agreed amount' with the insurer to reflect the vehicle's above-market price tag.

The same 'averaging' principle can apply to your property and contents cover as well, although many policies are based on the number of bedrooms with a contents total that is likely to be higher than their real value.

If you 'over-insure' by stating a higher value than the items are worth, you will pay more, but waste your money. You will not benefit on a claim – there is no 'reverse averaging' – and some insurers may be suspicious if you valued a £5,000 car at £10,000 when it comes to a claim, as they think you may have been dishonest.

66 If you under-insure, you could be hit by the 'averaging' trick and lose out, while over-insuring is a waste of money. 99

Insuring your home

Losing your home and what is in it adds up to the biggest conceivable financial loss for homeowners. Buildings insurance is compulsory for those with outstanding mortgages, but you do not have to use the insurance the lender sells.

The obvious advice for finding lower cost home and contents cover is to shop around. Buildings and contents cover could vary from £400 to £1,200 for the same house.

- Look at three comparison sites at least to give you an idea of what's on offer. Shopping around can be slow, so allow up to 30 minutes for each attempt with a call centre.
- Then phone a minimum of three insurers for definitive quotes.
- Don't be surprised if you are quoted a different premium when you make a real application – comparison sites often only give a rough idea because they cannot take into account the huge range of factors, which the company itself will want to know.

Start this process a month before your insurance is due. Remind yourself in your diary – your present insurer may only send out the renewal notice with next year's premium shortly before the end of the year to give you less time to find an alternative.

Don't be surprised if one insurer gives more than one quote – you might get a different amount online, going to a broker, calling the company or when insurers label their policies with other names – some big companies sell policies under a dozen or more labels. Many high street stores and supermarkets now sell insurance policies in their own names and these may be cheaper than the same products directly from the insurer because the store is willing to take a lower commission.

❝Some big insurance companies sell policies under many labels.❞

Money saving tip

Those with unusual homes – location, construction or features such as large amounts of land or outhouses – would generally do better to consult a specialist broker. For instance, there are insurance companies that specialise in rural properties such as thatched cottages. The website for the British Insurance Brokers Association (www.biba.org.uk) is a good place to start when searching for a specialist broker.

MONEY SAVING TECHNIQUES

Shopping around only works if you can compare like with like so give each insurer you try the same details. Although it is impossible to give accurate forecasts of how much you might save, these points should help you spend less on insurance by cutting out unnecessary cover.

- It is normally cheaper to arrange your property and contents cover with the same insurer with the same renewal date than covering each with separate companies. This can save 10–20 per cent.
- Go for the highest excess you can afford. This will reduce the size of premium that you pay – often by a significant amount.
- Insurers like safety. A home with good quality locks on doors and windows, smoke alarms, burglar alarms, security grilles and neighbourhood watch scheme is less prone to theft or damage. Insurers consider that these factors also show you are a responsible householder. There may be a discount – usually around 10 per cent, but make sure you use the locks and alarms.
- Insure your home for its rebuilding value, not its market value. A three-bedroom semi can cost £100,000 to buy in some areas and £500,000 or more in others. But the rebuilding costs will be similar. In the low-cost area, a rebuild could be more than the present value but in the high-cost postcode,

starting again after a total loss will be less than the market value. Insurers publish guidance based on the size and type of your home. Over-insuring is costly and pointless.

- Be clear about new expensive items that you have bought – and remember to take off any costly items you have disposed of.
- Consider a specialist insurer. If you have a very large or very valuable home and contents, you may be better off going to a specialist high worth insurer or broker.
- Look into no-claims discounts. Some home and contents insurers offer a no-claims discount each year. This may be attractive but it is the actual premium you pay that counts.
- High-value items such as cameras, laptops or jewellery that you regularly take out of the house should be insured separately – usually known as 'all risks'.
- Weigh up the cost of cover against what you will get if you claim (see the section on self-insurance on page 80).
- Decide if you want accidental damage cover, which can pay out if, for instance, you spill a bottle of wine on the carpet. This may depend on the quality of your furnishings. Some people regularly buy cover against putting their foot through the loft floor when they do not have a loft!
- Tell the insurer if you have lodgers or if you are going to be away for more than 30 consecutive days. You will pay more but you will not be penalised in the event of a claim.

- **Don't bother insuring the property if you are a tenant** – your landlord will do this. But your landlord will not cover your own contents.
- **Check on what's excluded.** Most policies exclude sheds, fences, outhouses, swimming pools, garden walls, garden plants and greenhouses. Some insurers will cover these – but at an extra cost.
- **Don't feel you have to buy from your lender.** Your lender may try to persuade you to buy cover from its own or its recommended insurer – either way it will get a cut. You are obliged to cover the property if you have a mortgage, but you can – with the exception of the odd special mortgage – go where you like. Your lender may demand a form of indemnity from the insurer (paperwork that effectively says the property is covered), but most insurers will do this for nothing.
- **If you are fifty plus, disclose your age.** Older people may sometimes pay less than younger folk. Retired people, for instance, are more likely to be in during the day, which discourages burglars and encourages safety while insurers believe that young people hold riotous parties that lead to the property and its contents being trashed. But all insurers work along these lines, so if you are older, you are not limited to one of the companies that markets itself at the fifty- and sixty-plus age group. There is nothing you can do about your age, but if you are part of a couple and one is older than the other, then the older person should arrange the insurance.
- **Don't stick with a student insurer.** Companies that compete for students may be expensive for you when you leave college and start working. Always do a comparison – some companies rely on your inertia to overcharge you.
- **Consider the value of legal expenses insurance.** This is an add-on usually costing £20 a year, which most home insurers try to sell you. Few ever use it although there are moves by some insurers to offer better value such as access to a website with legal forms, which you can fill in and then have checked by a qualified person. You will not need this if you have legal cover with a professional association or trade union membership or subscribe to Which? Legal Services.

❝ You must insure the property if you have a mortgage, but you can buy the cover where you like. ❞

 To find out more about Which? Legal Services, go to www.whichlegalservice.co.uk and see also page 212.

Insuring your car

Covering your car against third party risks - the injuries you cause to other people and the damage you do to their property - is obligatory in the UK. You need third party insurance before you can buy road tax for your car. It is an offence to drive without it.

Insuring your car is easier than insuring your home as there are fewer variables to take into consideration. Motor insurers - and there are over 100 in the UK - are primarily interested in the make, model and age of your car, your own driving record, your age, your occupation and where you live. Some may want to know if you live alone and how many miles a year you drive.

“ There are fewer variables to consider when insuring a car, but you'll need to choose the right level of cover. ”

AVOIDING UNNECESSARY CHARGES

In order to save money, take a look at the following suggestions.

Decide on the level of cover that's best for you

You have a choice between third party, third party fire and theft and comprehensive.

- **Third party** is the legal minimum. This will only protect the bodies and property of others.
- **Third party fire and theft** will also pay out if you car explodes in flames or it is stolen, but will not pay if you damage your car.
- **Comprehensive insurance** costs the most but will pay if you crash your car and the fault cannot be attributed to anyone else.

The Association of British Insurers is the trade body for the UK insurance industry. Its website has many free consumer guides on related subjects; see www.abi.org.uk.

Ask the expert

What level of cover should I buy?

Most drivers opt for comprehensive cover, but it is probably a waste of money if your car has an insurance value of around £1,500 or less. Young drivers may find comprehensive cover prohibitively expensive – so they should look into buying low-value cars. For instance, someone under 21 with a £1,000 car could pay as much as £2,500 for comprehensive cover but perhaps £1,500 for third party, fire and theft. As the maximum you would get if the car was a write-off is £1,000 (less your excess), it is a waste of money to have comprehensive cover. It's probably only marginally cheaper to get third party only – the insurer expects young drivers to cause high-cost injury and damage.

- **Uninsured loss recovery** (often called legal expenses cover) is also available, which provides you with help if your car is damaged by another driver and it is not your fault. This is not an alternative to comprehensive but can be useful, whatever level of cover you have, to chase drivers responsible for accidents that affect you.

Be aware of your age

Most motor insurers have two key age points – 25 and 75, although it can be 30 and 70 for some. The further you are below 25, the more they increase the rates. There can be a major saving if you put off car ownership for a year or two as between 17 and 25 rates fall quite quickly. Sticking to a push bike or using public transport between 17 and 22 could easily save £5,000 in insurance costs. A few insurers sell special policies for younger people, which are cheaper if they avoid driving between 11pm and 6am (or some similar hours), because the late nights and early mornings are peak times for accidents involving young people.

At the other end of the age scale, many insurers start to load extra on to the premium for age when you reach 75 years of age.

❝ You can save money by putting off car ownership for a year or two between the ages of 17 and 25. ❞

Buy a car that is suitable for your age

A 2.3 litre souped-up super-mini could cost twice or more in insurance as the lower specified 1.1-litre version of the same car when you are young. Alloy wheels, turbo-charging and special one-off paint finishes can also attract far higher premiums. All cars are rated by insurers on a 1 to 20 basis with 1 being the safest and 20 the least safe. A few, mainly in the £100,000 plus price bracket, are off the scale.

Your past record

Those people with a history of accidents or motoring offences attract higher premiums. But it is worth shopping around, especially if the offences are speeding where companies now differ greatly in their treatment of offending motorists because it is so easy to collect penalty points from roadside cameras.

❝ It is often worth shopping around if you have points on your licence as insurer's attitudes differ on this. ❞

Protecting no-claims bonuses

You can apply to have a protected no-claims bonus, so that in the event of you having an accident you do not lose this discount. But it comes at a cost, although not large if you have a good driving record. Is it worth it? Before signing up, look at what will happen if you do have a claim. Some insurers will put you back to nothing but others will only reduce your bonus by two years. And even if you keep your bonus, expect an increase next

time in the premium before the discount percentage. This is because you have claimed and your insurer knows you have blotted your record and will therefore be less attractive to other insurers.

Your occupation

Insurers have stereotypical ideas of jobs. They have a list of safe occupations and those it would rather not insure (or only at a very high price). But not all have the same rules – for instance, some insurers discriminate against all journalists (the explanation from insurers is that journalists are likely to drink, drive fast chasing a story, have a famous celebrity in their car and so on). Other insurers look at what the job actually entails so those journalists employed to work in offices and use public transport pay the same as other desk workers. Sometimes a new job title can help – recycling operative will be more acceptable than scrap metal dealer.

Business use

Using your own car for work means you must have 'business use' added to the standard 'social domestic and pleasure'. This can increase premiums – or you may get a reduction if you say you don't want business cover. If you don't use your car for commuting, tell the insurer as this could mean a lower premium.

 The Association of British Insurers can provide further information on the rating of your car or one you are considering buying; see www.abi.org.uk/carinsurance/search.

Moving from a company car to your own

If you want your own cover after driving a car that is not your own (belonging to your boss or to someone else in the family), some insurers will take your claim-free record into account. Others won't. Online comparison sites generally handle this badly or ignore it. So try a face-to-face meeting with a good broker.

Your annual mileage

You may be asked how many miles you drive each year. This is to give the insurer some idea of the risk. It is not legally binding. One or two insurers recently introduced policies based on mileage using satnav devices to check how far you drive. These may be better value for those who drive very little but, currently, there are too few of these to make a firm judgement.

Girls are cheaper than boys!

There is generally not much you can do about this! But women are rated as safer drivers than men for ages up to about 40 when the sex difference becomes virtually non-existent. You may, however, find that for a couple it is cheaper for the woman to be the main driver with the man named as the second driver.

Couples are better than singles

Couples, whether married or in long-term relationships, tend to have lower premiums than single people – this can apply across most age groups. Insurers believe those with partners take fewer risks than single people.

Multiple policy discounts

Many companies will offer you a discount if you have more than one policy with them, so it can be advantageous to insure a second or subsequent car in your household with the same company. But never take this at face value. A 15 per cent discount from a £400 policy (£340) is still more expensive than a £300 premium.

Higher excesses mean lower premiums

The excess is the amount you have to pay towards any claim. Provided you are prepared to shoulder a greater part of the risk by paying a larger slice of a claim, you will enjoy lower premiums. Many policies have a compulsory excess to which you can add a 'voluntary' excess. Ask the insurer for a range of quotes based on different excesses.

Where you keep the car

Insurers like cars kept in garages or driveways overnight, rather than being left on the street, and reduce premiums. But that does not mean you can't sometimes leave the car on the street – it may be impossible to avoid it if you are away from home.

❝ Insurers believe that those with partners take fewer risks, so couples get better rates. ❞

Car security features

Alarms and immobilisers should help prevent theft and so reduce your policy costs. Insurers will want to know the type of security you have. It is a waste of money to fit an expensive system to a low-cost car.

Foreign travel

If you have no intention of taking your car outside the UK, buying a policy with European cover is a waste of money.

Extra benefits

Some policies will supply you with a no-cost courtesy car if your own car is out of action following an accident. This can be useful to some – for others who might have another car or who are not car dependent, it is a waste of money. As with foreign travel (above) it is impossible to put a cost on benefits like this, but they have to be paid for in some way.

ADD-ONS

Motor insurers try to sell two sets of add-ons – the road rescue plan and legal expenses insurance.

Road rescue

Road rescue comes to your aid if you break down and should not be bought until you have compared the cost of a standalone plan. Whether you buy with a policy or standalone, you could well end up with the same person coming to sort out your car – the UK's two biggest motor insurers each own rescue companies. If you buy with your motor insurance, the rescue plan will run for the same 12 months as the car cover. This could mean giving up months from a previous scheme, which will usually be a waste of money.

Legal expenses insurance

Legal expenses insurance costs from £18 to £25 and generally only covers motoring problems including pursuing drivers who cause you an accident (known as uninsured loss recovery). Legal expenses cover may be worthwhile but check first that it is not included either in your household insurance policy or as part of membership of a trade union or professional association or that you subscribe to the Which? Legal Service.

❝ Road rescue and legal expense insurance are add-ons that you might choose to forego. ❞

Personal protection insurance

Covering your life or ensuring you get a payout if you suffer a serious illness or can't work due to sickness or accident, is big business. It's good advice for many but you have to shop around as almost all policies cover the same eventualities. Many people, however, do not need cover or need less than is 'recommended' by insurance sellers.

Life insurance sellers have a decades-old sales trick called the 'last widow card'. If they feel the 'prospect' (insurance jargon for the person who might buy) is only lukewarm at best, the seller will pull out an index card and say, ruefully, that 'this person was also not enthusiastic but he did eventually buy a policy. And what a good thing that was. For he died last week/month/year in a car/work/ sporting accident or from sudden cancer/stroke/heart attack and I have only just got back from giving the widow a big cheque from the policy proceeds. She is so grateful.' This is rarely true. But life insurance is an emotional subject and sellers will resort to anything to gain that commission.

Nevertheless, life insurance protection is worth considering if your demise (or serious illness) would mean your family going without – possibly without a home if they could not pay off the mortgage. But if you have no dependants or they could stand on their own financial two feet if you died and lost your income, or you have large amounts of life cover with your employment, then save your money.

> **Consider life insurance protection if it means your family wouldn't have to go without in the event of your death.**

 You will save substantial amounts by avoiding policies that offer life cover and savings or investment possibilities in one package. Types of policies to say no to include 'endowments' and 'flexible whole of life' as these offer less protection for your money because most of the premium goes into an often difficult to decipher high-cost investment. Many people have lost thousands from the 'endowment mortgage mis-selling scandal'. Investing and protecting should not be mixed together.

TERM INSURANCE

The principal variety of life insurance is called 'term insurance'. Here you pay a set premium for a specified period (usually 10–30 years) and, if you die before the policy expires, it pays a lump sum. At the age of 30 (in insurance jargon, you are '31 next birthday') you might decide you need £200,000 worth of cover for the next 20 years, by which time your children will be adult. You arrange a monthly premium, which you pay for the next 20 years. If you die, your family collects £200,000. If you survive the period, the policy expires worthless.

ℂ Premiums rise with the length of cover, so consider the age at which your children will be independent and when the mortgage will be paid off. 𝟿𝟿

PROTECTING AGAINST SERIOUS MEDICAL CONDITIONS

Scientific advances mean you can now survive many conditions that were previously fatal, such as heart attack, stroke, kidney failure and cancer. But if you contract one, your earning capacity may be hit. 'Critical illness' insurance pays out if you are brought down by one of a number of specified medical conditions. Many policies will also pay out if you die from other causes as well. The conditions are usually those in the Association of British Insurer's list so all policies should pay out for the same diseases.

Saving money on life and critical illness cover

There's a huge gap between best- and worst-value policies. And they all offer the same cover. So how do you choose?

- **Non-smokers pay less than smokers.** The gap widens as the age at which the cover is due to finish increases. A 19-year-old smoker buying ten years' worth of life cover will pay about 25–30 per cent more. But a 49-year-old smoker will pay around double that of a non-smoker. That's because you are much more likely to have your life shortened by smoking-related illnesses during your fifties than in your twenties. A 39-year-old smoker buying a 25-year policy would pay well over double the non-smoking rate because this plan would last until 64 when smoking deaths really start to become noticeable. If you give up smoking, you will need to be tobacco-free for at least a year (sometimes two years) before counting as a non-smoker.
- **The older you are at the outset,** the more you pay. Death rates increase with age, so insurance premiums go up as well.
- **The longer the period of insurance,** the more you pay. So don't cover yourself for more than you have to – key factors include the age at which any children become independent and when any mortgage is likely to be paid off.

- **Women pay less than men.** Women tend to live longer than men, although the gap is narrowing. At younger ages, women are less likely to die in an accident or act of violence than men. For younger ages, women pay around a sixth less while once in their forties and fifties, women pay about a third less. There is not much you can do about your gender but you can insure a couple, whether married or not, on a joint life policy, which is far cheaper than two separate plans. It only pays once, however – on whoever is the first to die or become critically ill.

MORTGAGE PROTECTION COVER

You can save money by buying life insurance (with or without critical illness cover), which is geared to a mortgage – known in the insurance world as 'declining term'. It works with a repayment home loan (but not one that is interest only), where the outstanding amount declines every year and reaches zero at the end of its set period. As the chances of payout grow as you age but the amount that would have to be paid out declines as you settle the loan, the premiums are cheaper.

❝ You can't change your gender but insuring a couple on a joint life policy is far cheaper than separate plans. ❞

INCOME PROTECTION COVER

This is often sold with a mortgage. It promises to pay out if your earnings stop due to unemployment or illness. This is a form of payment protection insurance and can add up to 7 per cent to your monthly repayments, money that would generally be better used in paying your loan off more speedily (see 'payment protection insurance' on page 97).

There is also a form of income protection called permanent health, which only pays out on illness. It is expensive and is generally only sold to the self-employed – it's the equivalent of the workplace cover that pays out when someone employed is off work due to sickness, which some employers offer. Permanent health policies pay out every month during illness until you are fit to return to work. You can also buy less expensive income protection plans, which usually limit payments to two years.

How much should I insure?

Look at a worst-case scenario, but you do need to count any life cover or long-term illness cover you might get from your employment, any return of pension plan contributions on your death, and state benefits to your family if you die or are seriously ill before making up your mind. And take the future earning potential of your partner into account as well.

Equally, remember that while inflation is currently low, any call on the policy is more likely to be when you are older than tomorrow. Take rising prices into account – at 3.5 per cent a year inflation, someone who thinks £100,000 is now enough would need to budget for £200,000 in 20 years' time.

Once you have decided on what you want to insure, how much and for how long, there is a bewildering range of premium levels for identical cover, whether it is life alone or critical illness plus life. The cheapest is often half that of the most expensive.

HOW FIT ARE YOU?

Provided you are in good health, have no previous medical conditions and have not visited your general practitioner for at least five years for any advice (other than minor ailments, contraception or pregnancy), then aim for the absolute cheapest for the policy you want. It is pointless to do otherwise.

But if you have a pre-existing condition or have been a frequent visitor to the doctor (and this can include depression), then the cheapest provider might well reject you as too high a risk. Low-cost insurers may be more likely to probe your medical record or send you off for a medical examination.

If you are turned down, you will need to alert other insurers of this. If you have doubts about your health record, consult a specialist life broker. This will usually cost you no more than going direct. There are a number of policies that are aimed specifically at those people who would not normally be insured by mainstream companies.

GO FOR RE-BROKE

Re-broking is where you abandon a life or critical illness policy to start again with a lower cost plan. This can save you money because premiums have fallen substantially over the past few years due to competition fuelled by the fact that we

Don't withold information

Don't try to save money by withholding information on previous illnesses. Many insurers cut back on their own expenses by not looking at the answers you give to the medical questions on the proposal form until you (or your family) claim. If they then find you either lied or failed to reveal facts, they can refuse to pay the claim for 'non-disclosure', even if the illness is not connected to what happened subsequently. An insurer is likely to look closely at anyone claiming a substantial amount at a young age – it's easy enough to find out if you have been smoking when you said you abstained. The insurer can then refuse to pay out.

❝ Re-broking can save you money because premiums have fallen over the past few years due to competition. ❞

Ask the expert

Can one company be cheaper?

No. Insurers often target a certain section of the population for a time. For instance, an insurer may decide it does not have enough risks among women aged 30-40 compared with men aged 40-50 so it might decrease rates for the females and increase them for the males.

However, some life companies nearly always appear as the most expensive in comparative tables. This could be because they are more lenient on those with past adverse medical histories.

Some more expensive companies may be more willing to offer cover on larger policies without obliging you to take medical tests. Or it might be that their sales model only targets the ultra rich or some other specialist niche so they show they are not interested in your business. Therefore they price themselves out of your market.

Furthermore, some of the extensive companies only sell through their highly remunerated sales force.

are living longer and some serious illnesses are now less frequent or more easily controlled by early medical intervention.

- Some large brokers will also rebate part of the commission they earn from the insurer into your premiums, giving you a further reduction. Always ask for this if it is not promised upfront.
- Re-broking can also give you the chance to increase the value of the policy – perhaps you now have more children or a bigger mortgage.
- It costs nothing to quit an existing policy – there are no exit fees – but don't give up on the old one until you are certain that you have been accepted on to the new insurance policy.
- Forget about re-broking if your health has deteriorated substantially as you will start off with far higher premiums on your new cover.

"Abandoning a life or critical illness policy and starting again is called re-broking. It can save you money because premiums have fallen. "

Insurances to avoid

The insurance industry's favourite phrase is 'peace of mind'. It uses this to justify policies that cost a lot, have high obstacles to climb before you can claim, pay out in comparatively few cases and then probably amounts you can afford out of your income or that of your partner, anyway. Here are some insurances you should consider avoiding.

EXTENDED WARRANTIES

These are typically sold along with electrical goods, ranging from state-of-the-art high definition big screen televisions to toasters and kettles costing under £10. They promise to repair or replace the appliance within a certain period in return for a premium (usually one-off). Some policies cover the lifetime of the machine – here you normally pay each month or each year.

The selling is usually high pressure – the salesperson is often remunerated more to push the insurance than to market the goods themselves because of the high margins on the insurance. Some high street retailers depend on these policies for the bulk of their profits.

Report after report – from Which?, Citizens Advice and the Competition Commission (as well as from organisations in the US and Canada) – point to one conclusion. These policies, which can add 20–30 per cent to the price of an item, are largely unnecessary and generally over-priced.

In most cases, the cover is limited to the 'youth' of the appliance, so on a computer you would find most policies are for three years – five years at most. The first year (and sometimes longer on more expensive items) is covered by the manufacturer's guarantee anyway and it is during this period – and into older age – that most appliance breakdowns occur. Some stores offer free guarantees past the first year while remaining competitive on price.

The best way of saving money here is to avoid these warranties altogether – if you are concerned about future bills, put all the premiums you would otherwise had paid into a savings account you designate for appliance repair. Some items are very cheap to replace, such as DVD players, Freeview set-top boxes,

 The website for Citizens Advice is www.adviceguide.org.uk, and the website for the Competition Commission is www.competition-commission.org.uk.

kettles and toasters. Kitchen appliances such as washing machines, cookers and dishwashers can be repaired – tests show it is cheaper to pay for these repairs when needed rather than pay out on extended warranty cover.

IDENTITY THEFT COVER

Banks and insurance companies now urge us to take out identity theft cover in case someone breaks into our bank accounts or credit cards. They often paint scary scenarios of what could happen without this cover and they give out very high figures of how many people are affected each year.

You can pay anything from £20 to £80 a year for this, but the benefits are very limited and the police and banks, using technology upgrades, have now reduced the incidence of ID theft.

Policies vary but a typical one pays for the following items:

- The cost of phone calls you have to make if you discover you are a victim.
- Legal action to prevent being sued by your bank.

- Helps to restore 'your good name' with credit agencies.
- Costs towards any unpaid time you take off work to deal with the matter.
- Costs towards loan application fees if you were turned down while your identity was compromised.

Very few of these policy benefits involve any real money – and few people have their identity stolen. The bottom line is that unless your bank can show you were complicit in some way in the fraud, the bank itself will meet your losses and put matters right.

Not even the most expensive policy can prevent you becoming a victim. You may be better off investing in a shredder.

PAYMENT PROTECTION INSURANCE.

This is extra money you pay on a loan or a credit card bill to provide financial help if you are out of work.

It is of little use if you are self-employed, on a short-term contract or work for a family firm because you will be excluded from claiming. But you won't necessarily be told this by the seller. And it is not much more use if you are employed. Insurers typically pay out between 20 and 25 per cent of what they take in as premium payments so the price is grossly exaggerated.

❝ Banks and insurers paint scary scenarios of what could happen without identity theft cover. ❞

Personal loan cover

If you take out a personal loan – say £5,000 over three years at a fixed rate – you will almost certainly be offered payment protection insurance (PPI). This will pay your instalments in those months when you are incapable of earning due to unemployment or sickness or accident.

Taking out this cover will increase the overall monthly cost of your loan by around 30 per cent – and it will effectively double the headline interest rate. You will not be told this. Nor will you be asked if you have a partner who could pay the loan if you could not. In some cases, it will be strongly implied that you must take out the cover if you are to get a loan. This is not so.

You could save a substantial sum by banking the loan cover amounts. If you lose your income, you will then probably have enough to pay for several months, giving you time to re-arrange your finance. And if you stay in work, then you will have a tidy sum to look forward to at the end of the loan period.

But if you buy PPI and succeed in claiming, very few people are out of work for that long that they get more back than they pay in. If you were incapacitated on a long-term basis, you might get an income from your employer or from social security. And if you have no income at all or very little, you should contact your bank and re-arrange the repayments.

The Financial Services Authority (FSA), the Office of Fair Trading (OFT) and Which? have attacked bad selling practices in payment protection insurance.

CREDIT CARD COVER

This promises to pay your credit card bill – or at least the minimum monthly amount – if you lose your job. It is sold in two ways: by hoping you will tick the box on the application (a few companies still have 'opt-out' boxes so you pay unless you deliberately say you don't want to) or, later on, by a phone call, which will appeal to your fear but also promise you 'it could cost nothing'. The 'free' aspect is true – provided you don't use the card and have nothing outstanding on it.

Otherwise, the card issuer will add between 0.6 per cent to 1 per cent of your outstanding balance each month. It does not sound much but over a year that's around 7–12 per cent in extra payments, which could be more than the interest rate quoted.

You will pay this even if you pay off the card in full and owe nothing. So if you sign up for this and regularly spend £500 a month on your card and then pay it off in full, you will be paying out up to £60 a year without any benefit whatsoever.

> **“ Taking out payment protection insurance will increase the cost of your loan and effectively double the interest rate, and there are better options available. ”**

MOBILE PHONE COVER

Typically costing between £60 and £120 a year, this is usually sold as an add-on when you take out a contract or buy a new phone. In the same way as extended warranties, mobile phone cover is more attuned to the financial needs of the retailer and the salesperson than to you. They'll sell you 'peace of mind' for 'less than 40p a day – and what can you buy for 40p?' But 40p a day is £144 a year – and that may be more than the cost of your phone.

Some policies are very limited. They will pay out for theft, but only if violence is used – pickpocketing and stealing from handbags does not count. Many will not pay out for accidental loss or damage.

Although they do not advertise it, many networks will replace your sim card free of charge if your phone is lost as they want to retain you as a customer. You could then buy a phone or use an old one. You can buy a cheap pay-as-you-go phone for as little as £30 and pay £5 to £10 to have it unlocked so your sim card works – or ask a friend or family member if they have an old phone they do not use. Networks may offer you a refurbished phone until the end of your contract as well.

You may be able to add a really expensive mobile phone on to your household cover in the same way as a camera or a watch.

One fear sellers play on is that someone will steal your phone and run up thousands of pounds calling overseas numbers, known as 'airtime abuse'. Phones can now be turned off centrally if you report their loss. Some networks can put a block on foreign calls.

> **❝ Some mobile phone cover policies are very limited and an expensive model could be added to your household policy. ❞**

ACCIDENTAL DEATH AND INJURY COVER

This pays out only if your death and injury are due to an accident. You do not get a payment for natural causes or self-injury or suicide or if you were 'reckless' or involved in a crime or are a member of the armed forces.

Banks often offer three months' free cover if you sign up for a direct debit for this policy, which pays out a set sum if you suffer death or injury in an accident. Sellers play on fear. For example, one company says: 'Accidents can happen to anyone at anytime, at work, in the home or even while travelling. It's not a pleasant thing to think about, but just consider for a moment what financial

 For more information on buying and using a mobile phone with money saving in mind, see pages 102-8.

protection do you and your family have in place should a fatal accident happen to you?' This particular policy covers £20,000 for £2 a month. More expensive policies may also cover injuries – so much for losing a leg, an arm, an eye or a finger.

Accidental death is rare – it happens less often than before thanks to improvements in car construction and medical advances. Figures from the Office of National Statistics show it is only a major cause of death among males aged 15 to 24. And £20,000 won't go very far. Furthermore, in many circumstances, the family of anyone suffering an accidental death or injury (such as at a workplace or on public transport) will be able to sue.

Life cover against all forms of death is usually better value – for instance a 30-year-old man in good health could buy a £100,000 policy from around £10 a month.

❝Accidental death is rare these days, and life cover against all forms of death will usually be better value.❞

Deal or no deal?

Small daily expenses such as mobile phones and transport can mount up to big sums across the year. Making the extra effort to hunt for bargains on these lower cost items can lead to a large financial reward.

Phones: talk more, pay less

The cost of chattering on the phone – or texting – has never been cheaper or more competitive. But if you stick with your present supplier, you could lose out on the best deals. This section looks at mobiles, landlines, broadband and how you can use your computer to gossip away for very little.

You could spend £150 a month on your total communication needs. Or you could buy the same for less than a third of that – giving annual potential savings of over £1,200.

MOBILE PHONES

Ten per cent of households now have no fixed landline phone – the percentage is far higher among younger people. Mobile phones now account for around a third of all voice calls. For a typical monthly mobile package of 500 voice minutes and 100 text messages, you could spend anything from £20 to £100. Which? tests show switching to the best mobile deal can save many users up to £120 a year.

Getting the best deal for your needs

Saving money on a mobile starts with working out what you want from your phone. Try to calculate how much you will use it and how – but always build in a bit extra as a cushion – it's amazing how much longer most phone calls take than you think (see opposite).

Whatever sort of user you are, always start with what you are likely to use on calling and texting. It's all too easy to buy into an unsuitable deal because you like the style or the colour or the camera on a particular phone.

> **Always start by identifying what sort of user you are to help avoid buying an unsuitable deal because you like the style or features offered.**

 Mobile phones aren't the only means of communication that you can save money on. See also landlines (pages 109-11), voice over internet protocol (VOIP) (page 111) and broadband (pages 114-15).

What sort of user are you?

Heavy user

- You tend to call for up to 1,000 minutes and work your way through 200 or more text messages a month.
- Will probably also use your phone for the internet and email.
- Will want the latest phones with as many communication features as possible and an all-encompassing contract giving state-of-the-art technology that allows you a huge amount of calling and texting.
- Expect to pay at least £40–£50 a month.

Medium user

- Monthly usage is around 400 minutes with around 50–100 texts a month.
- Probably will not use mobile internet facilities very often, but will be prepared to pay extra for occasional online mobile access.
- The best deals come from a monthly contract tailored to your usage.
- Expect to pay £15–£25 a month.

Light user

- Probably keep your mobile for occasional use – perhaps leaving one in your car in case of a breakdown.
- The best solution here is pay as you go (PAYG). Each minute of a call can be expensive – up to 35p on some tariffs – but if you don't use the phone, you don't pay for it.
- There are also a few 'hybrid deals', which combine some of the features of a contract with those of a PAYG.
- Expect to pay from under £1 a month for a little-used emergencies-only phone to well over £100 if you are on pay as you go but you use it as a main phone.
- If you are regularly spending £15 or more a month on PAYG, look at a contract phone unless the 'can't spend more than my credit' feature on PAYG is really important to you.

MONTHLY CONTRACTS

Phone shops are keen to sell you a monthly contract – it's their job to try to sell these first because that is their big earner. But check first that you need a monthly deal – pay as you go may generally be cheaper if your usage is under 50 minutes and 20 texts a month. Listed opposite are some advantages and drawbacks of monthly contracts.

> ❝Before buying a monthly contract check that you need it.❞

Negotiating a new contract

You are in a great position at the end of the contract to cut a new deal. Your network will want to keep you as it's always better for them to deal with an existing customer than try to find a new one. So threatening to go elsewhere is your strong point. Never let on that you are happy with your present supplier! You can always take your number with you to a new phone company in any case.

Always start this negotiation process well before the end of your contract – some contracts demand 30 days' notice of any change, even if your 12 or 18 or 24 months are up. Networks may let you commence negotiating up to three months before the deal terminates.

There are three choices with the 'customer retention department' (that's the people you get when you press the 'thinking of leaving us?' menu option).

1 Negotiate a new contract with a new phone. This should be better than any on offer to new customers, otherwise you might just as well take your number and business elsewhere.

2 Keep the old phone but demand far lower charges. Phone companies add in around £10 a month over a contract for the 'free' phone. Be prepared to negotiate a further tie-in period for this. Alternatively, agree to continue at the same rate with the same phone but demand a much better package.

3 Stay on the same monthly tariff as now but without a new phone – the main advantage of this is being able to walk away from the whole deal as you are no longer held in by a long-term contract. This is the least desirable outcome but it is what will happen if you do nothing. It can be useful, however, if you don't want to be tied down – maybe because you are leaving the country.

Be wary of 'phone resellers'. Many will phone or text you well before your contract ends with offers of 'upgrades'. Some of these deals are unsuitable and you could end up paying a lot more. They may even trick you into paying for two contracts at once - a total waste of money.

The pros and cons of monthly contracts

Pros

- You'll usually get a 'subsidised' (the adverts will call it 'free') phone – its cost is built into your tariff.
- You'll often have a wide choice of handsets – better ones come with more expensive contracts.
- You'll have a built-in bundle of calls and, generally, texts. So you won't have to worry about your usage – most phone companies allow you to check on how much of your bundle remains by text message or through a free call to the company.
- You could effectively pay 3p–5p a minute if you make full use of your inclusive minutes and texts instead of the typical 15p–25p or more a minute with a PAYG phone.
- You may be able to upgrade your contract before it ends if you want more minutes or texts.
- You'll be seen as a more valued customer – useful when you want an upgrade either of your handset or your contract or when you negotiate a new contract.
- If your phone is lost, damaged or stolen, many networks will give you a new one (or at least a refurbished one), especially if you are approaching the end of your contract and they want to retain your custom. It's often a question of asking.

Cons

- You'll have to sign a long-term contract. The majority of such contracts are now for 18 months but there are many for 12 months and a few, usually on the most expensive handsets, for 24 months.
- You won't be able to downgrade to a lower usage package without paying a penalty.
- You need a suitable bank account for the direct debit.
- You cannot usually carry over unused minutes and texts from one month to another.
- You cannot usually put the deal on ice if you go away for a period.
- Your free minutes do not work abroad (although there are exceptions, so it's worth researching the different suppliers if this is important to you).
- Some tariffs become expensive if you exceed your monthly allowance.
- If your phone is stolen or lost, you are responsible for any calls that are made on it until you tell the network to block the line.

PAY AS YOU GO (PAYG)

These are ideal for light users. In most cases, you top up the phone – over the internet or on the phone – from your debit or credit card, through some bank cash machines and (for cash) over the counter at a large number of convenience and other stores. PAYG phones are suitable for those under 18 (who can't sign a contract although many ask their parents to do so) and for anyone else who does not have a bank account or who does not want to be tied into a fixed-term deal.

All you need is a handset and a sim card to make it work. New PAYG phones are locked to one network. But you can often get the phone unlocked (£5–£10 at some phone shops or other stores including some street market stalls). Or you could use an old phone whose contract has ended – again get it unlocked so you can use the best network for your purpose. A number of retailers sell sim cards – around £5–£10 – but they may come with some built-in credit.

There can be big variations between PAYG deals. Some have weekend or off-peak discounts while others charge less for a call to a landline than to another mobile. So it's a question again of deciding on how you will use your phone before accepting any deal.

The pros and cons of PAYG

Pros	Cons
• The calls are more expensive per minute than contract calls but you are in control.	• You can run out of credit when you are making an important call.
• You cannot spend more than the amount credited to your line.	• It can be very expensive if you leave the light user category.
• You're not tied to a contract.	• Watch out for minimum call charges – even if you are not connected.
	• Avoid deals where you pay by the minute – by the second is fairer.
	• Avoid deals that require minimum monthly top-ups.

Half-and-half deals

Some phone companies now have contracts where you are on PAYG but you get lower cost calls if you contract to top up the phone by a minimum amount each month – usually £15–£25. These credits carry over to following months – useful if you make few calls one month but then a lot in another. Some of these 'hybrid' deals offer a 'free' phone at the outset.

SIM-ONLY CONTRACT

If you don't want or need a new handset, sim-only contracts are worth considering as the monthly fee is lower. You'll just be given a new sim card – you can ask for its number to be changed to that of your old phone.

You get some of the lower costs of a full monthly contract but without the tie-in so you can end it at 30 days' notice, even if you have just started.

ROAMING

This is phone company jargon for using your phone outside the UK (and that

> **There are big variations between PAYG deals with varying call rates and weekend discounts so be clear how you will use your phone before signing up.**

 To prevent unwanted phone calls, you can join the Telephone Preference Society for free: go to www.tpsonline.org.uk.

Cashback companies: beware!

Be doubly wary of 'cashback' companies that promise you low or even zero cost packages where you pay the full price but then apply to the company for a cheque, which returns all or part of what you have so far spent – this is called a cashback. A number of these companies have gone bust, leaving customers paying for a far more expensive deal than they bargained for. And other firms often rely on small print clauses to refuse cashback repayments. They may claim you did not send in the redemption certificate on time – and even when you show you sent it by recorded delivery, a few have even claimed there was only blank paper in the envelope. Once you break the terms of the cashback, you risk automatically going on to a far higher cost tariff and never going back to the original arrangement.

The major names in mobile phones have generally stopped using this charging method. But if you think you've been mis-sold in either of these ways, contact your provider, who should be able to advise you on what to do. The main phone networks have now become more aware of the problem.

 Never agree to any deal over the phone, especially if the re-seller has contacted you. Ignore text messages asking you to call a number to get a 'great new deal' or similar words. Treat statements like 'one day only sale' or 'I can only offer you this today' with contempt. Legitimate deals do not disappear overnight – and mobile packages have come down, and will probably continue to fall, in price in any case.

includes the Republic of Ireland). Your bundle of 'free' minutes or texts or the rate you are used to paying on PAYG does not apply (although there may be exceptions from time to time). Also, you'll not only have to pay a higher rate of up to £2 a minute to send calls, but you will also pay to receive calls and texts from the UK (or anywhere else). Phone companies have been ordered to reduce these costs in the European Community (they can nevertheless still be high), but that ruling does not apply further afield.

If you visit a country for any length of time and intend making calls mostly within that country, you would save by taking an unlocked phone and buying a sim card locally.

 To unlock your phone for free so that you can use it abroad, go to the website www.trycktill.com/eng/.

LANDLINE PHONES

You no longer need a landline or fixed phone – even for broadband – but calls are a lot cheaper than from mobiles and you can have a handset in every room of your home if you wish.

The days have long past when everyone was tied into BT and almost every phone was black. Now you have a choice of phone companies, often with packages that can include broadband or television. Or there are 'indirect services' where you dial a code (or a dialler – a special gadget that fits into your phone socket dials/adds the code for you) before certain numbers, such as overseas calls, so they become cheaper.

And there is the growing use of VOIP (voice over internet protocol) (see page 111), which can cut the cost of phoning abroad, by using your internet connection to make calls.

Unless your phone is used infrequently or mainly for incoming calls or just as a conduit for your broadband, it's probably best to look at a package on top of the basic line rental. It's a question of finding the best for your needs. These packages can include:

- Weekend calls free – pay for others.
- Off-peak and weekend calls free – pay for others.
- All calls free (see the box, below).

Also check whether there is a connection charge or if the calls are purely limited by time.

What counts as a 'free' number?

Numbers that are usually 'free'
- 0800 numbers.
- 'Geographic numbers': these are numbers that start with 01, such as 0121 for Birmingham, or 02, such as 023 for the Portsmouth/Southampton area. In time, geographic numbers will include the 03 numbers, which are being introduced in some parts of the country as phone companies run out of numbers.

Numbers that are not 'free'
- Premium rate calls.
- Numbers that start with 0844 and 0845 (even though these are billed as local call rate; nor do these numbers work for dial-up internet because dial-up is usually an 0844 or 0845 number).
- Numbers that start 0870 and 0871.

For more information about VOIP, how it works and some money saving advice, see page 111. For a more in-depth explanation of what '08', '07' and '09' numbers mean, see pages 112–13.

Calling overseas

It can be cheaper to call Perth, Australia, than Perth, Scotland, or New York rather than York. You just have to know how.

- **Look for specific destinations:** Most people use the phone to call a short list of numbers overseas – usually friends and family – so it's worth targeting your money saving towards those destinations. Deals that are good for Afghanistan are not necessarily best value for South Africa, while calling Italy has a different set of costs to phoning India.

> **❝It is worth targeting your money towards the overseas destinations you will want, and there are providers who offer free calls to some.❞**

- **Free calls overseas as part of the package:** Some companies, including TalkTalk and Tiscali, offer free calls to a number of overseas destinations – generally North America, Australasia and Western Europe – as part of their overall home phone and broadband package. So the two Perths should be for subscribers to these networks.
- **Use an indirect provider:** These route your phoning via their lines so once you have called the provider, the rest of your call is with it rather than BT

or another company. The quality of these lines can vary. There are two ways of doing this.

1 **Sign up for an account,** such as with www.18185.co.uk and www.Call1899.com . You dial an access number (sometimes this is done automatically by a dialler) and then you punch in the number you want. Your call is routed via this provider and a bill is sent out every month (usually online).

2 **Pre-pay for a bundle of minutes.** This pre-payment may often be via a premium-rate phone call, which will usually cost £15 – that's 10 minutes at the £1.50 rate. Or you might have to purchase a scratch card, which will also cost £10–£15. Once you have paid this fee, you should get a bundle of minutes either free or for a very small additional cost per minute. What you get in the bundle can vary immensely, with some firms specialising in certain destinations, such as Pakistan, Panama or Poland, where calls will be most competitive, leaving other countries more expensive. Again, you'll be given access numbers and codes. These are often advertised on public transport, on posters in convenience shops or in publications aimed at those coming from the country you want to call. You could find this brings down the cost of calling the United States from a standard 20p or so a minute to as little as 1p. If you don't use the card, you won't get a refund.

Calling the UK from overseas

You can often use a foreign prepaid phone card if you are overseas and want to call home from a public phone. They work in exactly the same way. Some cards, for example, bought in New York enable you to call the UK for less per minute than calling one block away in Manhattan.

You may also be able to use an internet café to make low-cost calls using internet technology.

Avoid hotel phones

Money savers never use phones in hotel rooms. Hotels can set their own rates and these can be very high indeed – over £1 a minute from some to overseas numbers. In addition, you may be billed a connection charge whether or not your call was successfully answered.

It's almost always cheaper to use a mobile in a UK hotel. Overseas, call boxes (especially with prepaid cards) are far better value.

And internet cafés can cost a fraction of using a hotel computer for emailing (although some hotels now offer free broadband if you have your own laptop).

❝ VOIP can save big bucks if you regularly talk to someone overseas for long periods, and all you need is some software and a special headset. ❞

VOIP

This stands for voice over internet protocol. It's a way of using your broadband and computer to make cheap (and in some cases free) calls to others who have a computer and VOIP facility. It can save big bucks if you regularly talk to someone overseas for long periods, especially if it's a destination that is outside a free home phone package.

All you need is a computer (anything built over the past ten or so years will work), an internet connection, some easy-to-obtain software and a special headset incorporating a microphone. The best-known software comes from Skype – other companies often use this but give it their own brand name.

Once you are set up on VOIP, you can call computer-user to computer-user free of charge and talk as long as you like as long as the other person has the same VOIP service. The downside is that both you and the person you are calling have to be around a switched-on computer, so it takes a little care to set up, but it's not insurmountable. Some families, for instance, might have a standing arrangement to talk to each other at midday every Saturday.

The quality of the call can sometimes be less clear than a conventional phone.

VOIP companies also offer calls to normal landlines – you just dial the number on screen. But these are rarely much of a bargain and they can sometimes be more expensive than a conventional landline. So you won't save much, if anything.

Numbers that could cost you more than you bargained for

0800

Free from landlines but typically up to 15p from mobiles, even where you have 'free' minutes.

0845/0844

These cost 3p–5p a minute from landlines and 10p–25p a minute from mobiles. 0844 tends to be more expensive. Firms using these numbers earn from 'revenue sharing', which means they can take part of the call cost.

0870/0871

So-called 'national rate' lines are, in reality, a more expensive revenue-sharing number. Landline calls to 0870 are around 8p in the day (when you are most likely to call them) while mobiles can go up to 20p a minute. The 0871 lines are even pricier – up to 10p a minute for landlines and 35p for mobiles.

0870 numbers are one of the biggest cons of our time. They are used by organisations that should be offering free calls – not earning pennies each minute, including the minutes you are on 'hold' listening to music you'd rather not hear. Some big banks use them for their complaints departments – they reckon no one is going to spend pounds on a call if their complaint is relatively small and, if they do, the bank earns from it. Some mail order companies use them as well. Here are some ways of getting around 0870.

- The website saynoto0870.co.uk has a good collection of alternative geographic numbers that will cost less or nothing if you have a landline or mobile package with inclusive minutes. It also covers other numbers such as 0844 and 0871.
- Websites often have a geographic number for callers from overseas; try that instead as it will usually lead to the same people.
- Letter headings and websites may have fax numbers, in which case send a fax if you have access to a machine and demand the company calls you, especially if it is a complaint about their services.
- Complain about the high cost line and demand they call you back if they want your business.
- Send an email.
- Some mail order companies have freepost addresses so you can buy by post.
- Avoid organisations that use these numbers as far as you possibly can.

07

Numbers starting 07 followed by any number other than 0 are mobile phones. The costs of calling these depends on which phone you are calling from and which mobile network the recipient is on. It is very complex with scores of possible combinations.

070

These are 'personal numbers', which can reach their owners anywhere whether they are at home, at work or out and about. They can cost up to 50p a minute – so avoid! These numbers have never been widely used in the UK, however.

09

These are premium rate calls, which can cost up to £1.50 a minute from landlines and £2.50 from mobiles. Regulator PhonePayPlus (www.phonepayplus.org.uk) puts limits on the duration of most of these calls. Most of the call money is kept by the information or content provider. These are used by legitimate enquiry lines but also by so-called lotteries where all you are likely to win is a low value piece of jewellery or almost useless digital camera.

“ Be aware of what each prefix represents and then you can choose whether or not you wish to dial these numbers. ”

BROADBAND

Broadband connections are now in around half the households of the UK. Prices are falling and generally the quality is rising. But don't be fooled by the quoted speeds such as 8Mbps (megabits per second). These are usually maximum speeds rather than the standard delivery and the real speed may be less than half that which is quoted.

When you sign up to a broadband package, you will usually be sent free software, and a free wireless modem also comes with many packages.

 Some companies have download limits – others say they don't but if you leave the machine on all day and all night as you download film after film, you might find that the 'fair usage' clause kicks in. This allows the company to curtail your signal (or tell you to go online in the less used night-time hours), but no one really knows what the limits are or which company applies what. Threatening to move to another provider can be effective if you think that your provider's claim that you have breached 'fair usage' is unfair.

> ❝ The high speed quoted is usually a maximum and the reality is slower. ❞

Add-ons to look out for

- **'Free' landline calls** (including some to overseas destinations), which are available with many deals.
- **Bypassing BT altogether** so you only pay one bill per month. Expect to pay £15 a month for this with a low speed download, £20 with a better broadband connection.
- **Provision to watch** a number of TV stations via cable or satellite (although these may be the stations that are free to air on Freeview, leaving you to pay extra for premium channels such as sports or films).

Budget £25–£30 per month for phone, broadband and some TV content.

 There are many comparison sites for broadband charges on the internet, but before going online, check out pages 17–22 so that you don't get caught out.

There are lots of 'half-price' deals around so some providers advertise as little as £7.99 a month in big print. But don't be deceived. These are usually for the first three to six months only. The only fair comparison is the total cost over the contractual life of your package. And always compare like with like – especially important if your deal includes television.

Contracts now tend to last 18 months so you have to be sure before you sign. Ask if you can drop out without penalty after one to three months if the service does not work well for you.

Money saving tip

If you get on well with your neighbour, you could share your wireless broadband signal and divide the costs. One wireless router and connection can often serve a small block of flats as well. Provided everyone uses normal encryption and passwords, there should be no security problems, but you must check all terms and conditions carefully before entering into such a share.

❛❛ Don't be deceived by half-price deals as they usually only last for the frst three to six months. You should look for the total cost over the contractual life of the package. ❜❜

Which? Computing offers you honest unbiased reviews of the best (and worst) new technology, problem-solving tips from the experts and step-by-step guides to help you make the most of your computer. To subscribe, go to www.computingwhich.co.uk.

Transport

The cost of phoning may have fallen, but the expense involved in travelling continues to rise and rise. This section looks at ways to save money on the move.

TRAINS

You can pay more to travel from London to Manchester by train than it costs to fly from London to New York. But amidst some of the most confusing fare structures in the world, you can find some real bargains.

There are literally dozens of fares on popular longer-distance train routes, ranging from unrestricted first class to standard-class tickets you have to book ahead. Fares are forever changing – sometimes as much as three times a year on some lines on so-called 'unregulated fares'. Some fares, including Savers and season tickets and other tickets used by commuters, are regulated so annual increases are limited to a formula (usually based on inflation plus a percentage), but most, including Standard Open and advance purchase tickets, are unregulated.

With some pre-planning, you can travel the same journey as another passenger for a fraction of what they are paying. The lowest 'walk-up' return fare from London to Liverpool at the time of writing is £59.70 if you avoid the morning peak. Or you could get a first-class return for £322.

Use the internet to check prices

Which? has found that information given over the phone and at stations does not always lead to the best value fares, so it's best to use the internet to check prices (and the times of trains while you're at it). Also, some tickets may only be available online – go to www.thetrainline.com or one of the train companies' websites.

Planning is easiest on the National Rail website (see below). Besides showing train times and connections, it also gives the range of available fares. Although it doesn't sell tickets itself, it can link you through to the relevant train company's website or an online ticket retailer (also see below).

 The National Rail website is at www.nationalrail.co.uk and for an online ticket retailer, go to www.thetrainline.com.

Always book as far ahead as you can (normally six weeks)

This is especially true of travelling longer distances (from 50 miles upwards). The standard no-restriction single from London to Liverpool is £102.50. If you are happy to book four weeks ahead and travel on a train leaving London at 10.15am you can travel for as little as £12.50. Don't forget that the cheapest fares may only be valid on the one train shown on your ticket. If you miss it, you will have to pay the full price – and lose what you've already paid. If this worries you, go for the more flexible saver ticket instead.

The best deals – those really cheap tickets that are advertised – go first. Apex and Super Apex fares are often limited in number per train so you have to be quick. Some low-cost tickets cannot be bought within seven days of travel so you have to buy before that.

Try to avoid peak periods

These are usually between 7 and 9am and, in some areas, between 4pm and 7pm, Monday–Friday. Prices are higher at these times. On some journeys, train companies are starting to bring in a 'shoulder' – a still pricey period either side of the peak times, further squeezing bargain hunters.

Find out if you qualify for a discount card

- **Young person's railcard:** If you are aged 16–25 years, you qualify for one of these. You do not have to be a full-time or part-time student as this is based on age. But full-time students over 25 qualify as well. This costs £20 a year (but sometimes given away with student banking packages). The card gives a reduction on most standard (second)-class fares but not on certain routes, such as the Heathrow Express or on season tickets or some heavily discounted tickets.

- **Senior railcard:** If you are 60 or over, you can buy one these for £20 a year. This gives one-third off a range of fares including some first-class travel. These tickets rapidly pay for themselves if you travel longer distances. For instance, the Saver return ticket (which cannot be used at peak times) from London to Manchester costs £59.50 – and with a railcard, regardless of whether it is a young or senior person's railcard, it comes down to £39.70, so having the £20 card for a whole year is almost paid for by one journey. The full Open return fare for this journey would be £219, with a railcard it would be £146.

- **Network railcard:** People in London and the southeast use trains more than those in other parts of the country. Whatever their age, they can buy a Network card. For £20, this gives one-third off weekend travel and one-third off longer journeys off-peak in the week. It also allows for another three adults and up to four children aged 5–15 to travel with you at discounted rates. It is not as useful as the Young person or Senior cards. It is not worth buying if you qualify for either of these other cards because they offer the whole country, not just the southeast of the country.

- **Family railcard:** For £20 a year, there is a one-third reduction on adult fares and 60 per cent off children's fares. There has to be a child travelling with you.
- **Group save:** Some lines offer four tickets for the price of two, which reduces fares.
- **One-day travelcard:** If you are travelling after 9.30am or at weekends to London and are planning on travelling around London by public transport (or you are just travelling around London for the day), buy a one-day travelcard.
- **Oyster card.** If you are travelling by tube or bus in London, it's a real money loser to buy tickets as you go. One underground stop in central London is now £4 – the most expensive metro in the world. And one bus stop will set you back £2 – and that's assuming you find a bus that takes cash (many in the central area do not, including most night buses). Instead, do as most Londoners do and get an Oyster card – you can do this online (see below) or get the card from many convenience shops and tube stations. The Oyster card cuts the central zone fare to £1.50 and the bus

to 90p. You pay £3 for the card but you can get that back should you no longer need it.

You don't have to buy a return ticket

Two singles can sometimes work out better value – especially if one journey is during peak time and the other off-peak. Again, check this out on the national rail or trainline websites. The best single ticket bargains can usually be booked from up to 12 weeks before travel.

> **❝Railway companies are crafty and charge the whole journey according to the starting time.❞**

Journey splitting can be the route to saving cash

The most expensive rail journeys are those made in the morning starting at the peak time. But if you're going a long way, a fair part of the journey could be in off-peak time. The railway companies are crafty, however. They charge the whole journey according to the starting time.

So you have to be craftier. Armed with the fare information on the internet, try to divide your journey into two and only

---

 To buy an Oyster card online, and top it up, go to the Transport for London website: www.tfl.gov.uk, or oyster direct at https://oyster.tfl.gov.uk.

pay the peak fare for part of it. For instance, Exeter to Manchester may only be peak as far as Bristol. If you go from London to Newcastle, you might be better off splitting your journey at Peterborough with the second portion off-peak. Depending on the route and the time of day, you could save anything from £20 to £50.

This is quite legal. You buy your tickets online or from your local railway station. The only proviso is that the train stops at the station or stations where each ticket starts.

Anyone with a London area season ticket enjoys travel at no extra cost in all the zones for which the ticket is valid. So if your normal journey is from north London to central London but you want to go to the south coast, don't pay for the first part. Ask for a ticket to your destination from the 'edge of zone six' (or whatever zone your normal season ticket takes you to). This could save you about £4–£5 on a return ticket – enough for a coffee and pastry on the train.

Annual season tickets

These can save money for regular travel. Most are based on the price of 40 weekly season tickets, giving you 12 weeks of free travel (assuming you do not take holidays).

Most annual season tickets give Gold Card benefits. Here holders are entitled to additional benefits and discounts:

- Your friends and family can travel with you and save one-third off the price of most standard fares at weekends, on public holidays and after 10am Monday–Friday.
- Four children may accompany you for just £1 each.

Don't forget that many employers offer interest-free loans for season ticket purchase. The interest benefit will generally be tax-free, provided it is less than £5,000.

Car sharing

Some stations offer free parking if there are three or more people in a car.

Money saving tip

Long-distance coaches often have heavily discounted seats in January and February.

❝Season tickets can save regular travellers money and many employers offer interest-free loans for their purchase.❞

 For more information about interest-free loans from your employer and other perks, see pages 176–82.

" Save motoring costs by sharing journeys, driving slower and more smoothly, and turning off the air conditioning when not needed. "

CARS

Other than homes, cars are most people's biggest single spending item. The biggest saving is to do without, but if you need a car – and millions do – then you can cut down your expenses.

Start with the big items

The biggest cost for most car owners is depreciation – the fall in a car's value as it gets older. Many cars lose half or more of their value over the first three years, including a big chunk the moment the new car leaves the showroom. You not only lose money, you may also be paying for it through a finance plan.

Look at how you drive

Many costs such as insurance, road tax and MOT-testing are fixed – you have to pay them whether you drive 2,000 or 20,000 miles a year. But you can save money on fuel, which at £1 plus a litre, is the biggest single cost you can easily control. Here are some ideas:

- **Drive more slowly.** Stick to the legal limit of 70 mph and save up to 4p a mile in small cars – more on gas guzzlers. This would save you around £8 on a return to Birmingham from Liverpool. If you can drive even slower, your fuel costs drop again. The Slower Speeds Initiative (a group founded by a number of cycling, walking and green organisations) says that driving at 50 mph instead of 70mph can cut your fuel bill by 30 per cent, though driving at town speeds will push up your consumption again.
- **Check tyres often** (at least once a fortnight, more often if doing high mileage). Under-inflated tyres can add 8 per cent to fuel bills and are likely to lead to uneven wear and premature failure, costing you even more than they would otherwise. And they're dangerous too.
- **Balanced driving.** Approach bends at an appropriate speed, taking a wide, balanced line, decelerating into the

 For more details on how to minimise depreciation - and how to make sure you get the best credit package for your needs - see pages 126-7.

bend. As you reach the crown of the bend, accelerate smoothly out into the straight beyond. In bends with clear visibility, take the straightest (most balanced) line.

- **Changing up and down the gears.** Doing this at the right time can save up to 25 per cent on fuel costs. So don't race away from one set of lights only to brake sharply at the next. This wastes fuel and will also cost you in increased wear and tear to the brakes. Change gear early in traffic and stay in the appropriate gear for your road-speed. Don't race the engine in too low a gear, but also don't labour the engine in too high a gear (this will waste un-burnt fuel and wear the engine unduly).
- **Don't skimp on regular services.** This is a false economy and may leave you stranded, too.
- **Only use a roof rack or bike rack when essential.** A fully loaded roof rack can add up to 30 per cent to your fuel bills.
- **Don't keep stopping at petrol stations and topping up.** It is time wasting and a constantly full tank also costs much more to drive around because of its weight.
- **Switch off the air conditioning** when it's not needed – it can add up to 10 per cent to your fuel costs.

- **Two in a car costs less than two cars.** Sharing a car on a journey divides the cost of the fuel and reduces congestion. Consider sharing for school runs, too.
- **Try walking, cycling or taking public transport** wherever possible. Walking or cycling briskly could also save on gym bills!
- **Avoid gadgets** that claim to save you big percentages on fuel bills. For example, a fuel-saver that has been advertised fits onto the fuel line and supposedly cuts consumption by 30 per cent. You are unlikely to be shown genuine proof they work.

Some supermarkets sell fuel as a 'loss leader' – they offer deals on petrol and diesel to persuade you to spend in excess of £50 or £60 at the checkout. And fuel is often cheaper at these sites anyway. Store up big non-essential purchases so you qualify for the typical 5p a litre reduction. This would save you £3 on a 60-litre purchase.

Towns where two or more superstores are close together and compete on fuel prices are often much cheaper than surrounding towns as independent fuel retailers also have to reduce prices to match the superstores. To find the cheapest fuel in your area, have a look at the handy comparison website www.petrolprices.com.

 For car sharing ideas, check out an online service such as www.liftshare.com or www.nationalcarshare.co.uk. Look, too, into car clubs such as Streetcar, WhizzGo and Zipcar. Some local councils/community groups also run not-for-profit car clubs.

SAVE MONEY ON FLIGHTS

More people fly more miles than ever before, attracted by adverts promising flights for 1p or even nothing. Many of these adverts are controversial as they fail to show the real price of your ticket. Some show very low fares leaving the UK but as the tickets are single, coming back could be pricier.

Before you book your flight, check that you have the full costs of your travel. This can include:

- The fare
- Premium rate phone lines
- Booking costs
- Credit card fees
- Insurances (some airlines demand you 'untick' this item when booking online)
- Air passenger duty
- Fees to check in baggage
- Meals on the plane (avoid wherever possible and take a sandwich).

Airlines have to make money somehow. On top of this, add in transport costs (or car parking) if you are using airports that are less accessible. For instance, someone in Birmingham who sees a cheap flight from Southampton will need to add in the cost of a railway return ticket – around £60 – while a traveller to Copenhagen taking a cheap flight with Ryanair will end up in Malmo in Sweden. Expect to pay around £6 for a bus journey from that airport to the Danish capital.

So, make sure you know the total price, including taxes and all other charges before committing to the booking. Also be sure that you know how much you will be charged for using a credit or debit card before deciding how to pay (or even whether to fly with the airline). But remember that using a credit card may give you protection against airline bankruptcy that you would not get with a debit card. If you book directly with a foreign airline, you won't get the same protection as dealing with a UK carrier.

Read the airlines' conditions before committing to the booking. Not for nothing do the airlines make you tick a box to say that you've done this!

- **Parking at airports** is very pricey. There are a number of firms that have long-term facilities near major airports – find them by putting 'long-term parking' plus the name of your airport into a search engine. These usually arrange transport to the departure area.
- **Avoid money changing facilities** at airports if at all possible – they are rarely good value.

> **!** Always check all the details on an online site before clicking OK – many tickets cannot be changed or refunded or you might have to pay a fee that can cost more than the ticket itself so it would be a waste of effort applying for a refund.

Ask the expert

Can I really fly for 1p?

Yes, although only occasionally. Some airlines would rather fill up a flight with people travelling for nothing – even absorbing air passenger duty – than flying empty. They reckon they can make money by selling meals and drinks onboard, charging for luggage and seat reservations, charging for credit card bookings and hoping that ticket buyers buy the optional travel insurance. On top of that, some even use £1.50 a minute phone lines if you need help. And even if you go out for 1p or less, you may find it far more pricey to come home. So – yes – there are some bargains around. But don't necessarily expect them at your most preferred travelling time.

- **Don't pay outrageous extra banking charges** when you use plastic overseas. Most cash machine cards add a fee for each transaction plus 2.75 per cent of the transaction value if you take money out overseas. Nationwide is the only high street bank not to impose these charges. The Post Office-branded Mastercard does not add a percentage for credit card usage overseas. Credit cards from Liverpool Victoria and Saga do not impose charges within the European Union.

Money saving travel hints

- Always shop around for air tickets.
- Try holiday comparison sites.
- Booking early is usually better than last minute.
- Travelling off-peak (the middle of the night or the middle of the day or the middle of the week and avoid school holiday periods if possible) is always cheaper and the more restrictions you accept on your ticket, the better value it will be. So be prepared to be flexible – or pay for the privilege of flying when you want to.

For holiday comparison sites, try www.traveljungle.com or www.travelsupermarket.com if you are interested in a package deal – these should find the best deal quickly.

- **Avoid the school holiday con.**
  Package holidays go up during school holidays including half-term breaks. And so do many 'budget' air fares. Avoid these periods where possible. But if you want to travel during school holidays, non-UK airlines may be worth trying. It's also worth considering 'unbundling' travel and hotels. For instance, a package week to New York over Easter from a UK agent can cost substantially more. But airfares from London to New York do not go up. Nor do hotels in the US (where Easter is a religious festival and not a major holiday) increase their prices.

Package holiday or independent travel?

Making this decision really comes down to a matter of taste and where you go. Package tours are generally better value when it comes to the most popular resort destinations. Hotels often have little or no spare space because all their rooms are pre-booked often months ahead by tour companies, who then have to fill them. As an independent traveller, you won't find too many bargains.

Package holidays can often fall dramatically in price in the week or two before departure. If you can travel at short notice – especially if outside of school holidays – you can find some bargains as tour operators have to get rid of the air tickets and hotels they have pre-booked. They would rather get £200 instead of the brochure price of £400 than nothing at all. But you cannot generally be too choosy at this late stage.

For other destinations, such as big cities or unusual places, independent travel is usually a better idea. But don't forget, you'll have to do some work on research, and costs, such as transfers from airports, will be an extra – they are included in packages. Independent travel also allows you to set your own agenda.

❝ If you can travel at short notice, you can get a bargain, but you can't afford to be too choosy about where you go or how you get there. ❞

 For more information on the best value for travel insurance, see pages 78-9.

Pay less, get more

Expensive items – known as 'big ticket' – such as cars and home improvements offer the biggest scope to money savers. But they could also be money losing traps. This chapter looks at purchases small and big, offering strategies ranging from haggling to how to get rid of that home improvement salesman who intends being a fixture in your front room.

Buying cars

For many people, the car is the most expensive item on their monthly budget after the roof over their head. But you can easily save thousands – if you know how. It is always worthwhile saving money on motor insurance or cutting fuel bills by sensible driving. But the biggest item of outlay for most car owners is the car itself.

Whether you buy a Ford, a Fiat or a Ferrari, your most important cost is the money tied up in the vehicle and depreciation – the fall in the car's value as it ages.

Which? Car, the annual car guide from Which?, gives running costs in pence per mile for new cars over the first three years and 36,000 miles of the vehicle's life. Many readers are shocked by these figures, which can top £1 a mile (for many luxury cars, and some 4x4s and sports cars). These include fuel, servicing and tax but, most vitally, they include depreciation. The moment a new car leaves the showroom, it loses value – often thousands – and many car owners count themselves lucky if they get back half what they paid after three years.

Depreciation is a fact of car-owning life that continues until the vehicle reaches a substantial age. But you can fight back against depreciation.

❝ Depreciation is a major cost but some names hold their value better than others. ❞

- It can often make sense to for 'premium' brands. It may not always be deserved but some brands are more in demand and hold their value better. It takes a long time for a car's brand image to turn around.
- Cars with a reputation for simple, low-cost maintenance tend to keep their value better.
- Diesel cars often hold value better than petrol engines, but are usually more expensive to run.
- Estate cars are often more in demand in the second-hand market than saloon cars.
- Go for the simplest model in the range. The extra a new car buyer pays for metallic paint or air conditioning rarely works through into the second-hand market, where buyers are less fussy about finishes or gadgets, though such extras might make the car easier to sell.
- Pay less in the first place. The next buyer does not know what you paid for it – she or he will pay what it is worth whether you got a discount or paid list price.

Money saving tip

If you buy a new car, check that your insurance will offer the price you paid rather than the depreciated value that occurs once it leaves the showroom if it is stolen or is written off during the first year. You may have to pay extra premiums for this.

BUYING NEARLY NEW

Dealers often sell cars with just a thousand or so miles on the clock at substantially lower prices than list. These come with the remainder of the warranty so you might get the three years less perhaps two or three months, although nearly new generally refers to any car up to 12 months old, so the warranty may have just two years left. The saving you will make should more than offset any loss on the warranty period – many warranty faults show up in the first few thousand miles anyway.

Where do dealers get them from? Some are last year's models – they want to be rid of them so they can feature newer cars in the showroom. Some are ex-demonstrators – cars that have been used to show prospective purchasers and give them a test-drive. And some might be surplus cars from hire companies. And some are really 'new' – they come with 'delivery' mileage only – this is a way dealers have of reducing prices without being seen to cut the list prices of their new cars. Don't be afraid to buy a pre-registered car if the discount is substantial, but bear in mind you will become the second owner listed on the logbook, which has a slight effect on future resale values.

Nearly new cars will depreciate, but not at the same percentage rate as a new car. The next owner will not know whether you have paid £12,000 or £10,000 – you will still be offered the same amount when you sell.

> ❝ Buying nearly new allows you to buy substantially below list price, with plenty of warranty to run. ❞

IMPORTING CARS

A decade or so ago, there was a big gap between UK car prices and those in Europe, so some people imported cars from the Continent (or sometimes Ireland). These came with the UK's right-hand drive and other specification necessities. But the gap in prices now is either narrow or non-existent. Unless you want a specific car that is only available in overseas markets, any gains from importing are small once all the work and expenses are counted into the calculation. These days, about the only worthwhile imports are cars at the very top of the market, which are not normally sold in the UK. These deals can take months and are probably for the price-unconscious.

Haggling hints

The hardest part of haggling is deciding you want to do it.
You need to get over two psychological barriers.

1 The worry that you'll offend the salesperson. Don't worry about this as they are trained to deal with rejection. They won't worry if they overcharge you.

2 Your own fear of rejection. How many car dealers are there? How many home improvement companies are there? Take a look in your Yellow Pages. If you are dismissed out of hand by many, then perhaps you are asking for too much – probably 10 per cent off a car is the most you'll get, but it could be double that or more on a home improvement project. If you don't ask and don't try, you will not save money.

> **"** Salespeople are trained to deal with rejection. They won't be offended if you walk away or haggle, and they won't worry if they overcharge you. **"**

> **"** Having a range of quotes at your fingertips will help you cut a better deal. Don't accept the first offer of reduced price and upgrade package: the dealer can always do better. **"**

Here are some pointers:

- Always set yourself a limit on how much you will pay. Be realistic, and if you are buying a car, don't forget you'll need to pay tax and insurance.

- Research the market – quoting what's available elsewhere has a big effect. Check on prices and, for a car, check depreciation rates using the Which? online Car Buying Guide (see box at bottom of page 130) or one of the monthly price guides.

- Treat the first haggles you try as a test session. See how they react.

- Always shop around – dealers expect you to haggle. Even if you like your local dealer as a safe and convenient place to buy, having other quotes at your fingertips will help you cut a better deal. Don't just accept the reduction and/or upgrade packages from the manufacturer. The dealer can always better this as they will have their own margin to play with, too. Haggling can cut 5 per cent or more from the price. Ask for the 'best price' and quote lower online prices at them.

- Never be rude – the seller has to emerge with some money and some dignity.

- Home in on imperfections – this works on second-hand cars.

- Look disinterested – walk away but leave your contact number in case the seller changes his or her mind.

- Tell the seller that you have other firms to see – name them.

- Asking for free upgrades as an alternative to lower prices can work – for instance, many bike shops offer 10 per cent off new bikes. But some would rather add in a £20 accessory (such as lights or a lock or a carrier rack) on a £200 bike – it costs them less than £20 in cash, but it has the same effect for the customer.

- Second-hand car buyers can negotiate on the length of the MOT and road tax.

- Expect periods of silence. Don't back down. The longer the silence, the better it is for you.

- Don't agree to split the difference between what they want and what you want to pay unless you are sure it is a good bargain at that price – split and split again where necessary.

- If you need finance, always take quotes from a number of sources rather than just accepting the package the dealer offers.

- Never, never show that you are in love with what is being sold.

- Learn from rejection, but don't be put off.

USED-CAR BARGAINS

Anyone buying a used car wins from depreciation, especially as cars are now more reliable than they used to be. You can find bargains, especially if you are not too choosy about the model or the finish.

- Company car fleets are smaller these days as the company car is not the tax-saving perk it used to be. But there are still many around – cars from this source may not have a super specification or alloy wheels or leather seats, but they are usually well maintained and are often sold at bargain basement levels at auctions and on internet used car lots.
- Big cars lose their value faster than small cars. They will often have lower second-hand purchase prices (and so lower financing costs), but higher fuel, maintenance and insurance costs. Big cars can save money for low-mileage users for who fuel prices are not so important.
- Look for less popular cars or those that are no longer in manufacture. Some colours are less popular – green is considered unlucky by some drivers so green cars might be cheaper on the second-hand market.
- Cars with a reputation for unreliability may be cheaper. This may matter less

Money saving tip

The best time to buy a second-hand car is in December when most potential purchasers are more interested in Christmas shopping. And as few people are attracted to an open-top or convertible car in the late autumn or winter weather, prices can fall-offering bargains.

to some who do not need a car for daily transport or who are confident of their ability to repair cars or who do low mileage. The *Which? Car* is a good guide to reliability – or otherwise.

❝ Ex-company cars will be well maintained and are often sold at bargain prices. ❞

FINANCING YOUR CAR PURCHASE

Paying for the car involves a lot of money and few people can just take the cash out of their bank account. Dealers are keen to sell finance packages – but you need to get several quotes, and look at what your bank can do for you.

 To check the Which? online prices and depreciation rates, go to www.which.co.uk and click on the 'cars'. You do, however, have to subscribe to Which? to access this information.

Ask the expert

Should I buy an old banger?

Getting an old banger – something aged over ten years and costing less than £1,000 (or even less) – can be a great way to cut motoring costs if you are not too fussed about what the car looks like and you can live with the prospect of not having a working car from time to time. It makes sense if the car will not be used that often or you are on a low budget – the cost of credit will be low as well.

Take the mechanical parts. In many cars, the engine, brakes, gearbox, clutch and steering last far longer than the trim and body appearance. If you buy a car for £500, you know your depreciation is limited to £500 – some new cars at the higher end of the market lose this much every month. That's a worst-case scenario assuming a major mechanical failure that will cost more to repair than the car is worth. If that happens, sell it for scrap and buy another. In fact, old bangers are often sold for just as much as the owner paid for them or they are kept for so long they are virtually run into the ground.

Insurance is a saving, too, as there is no point in buying a car at this price and insuring it with comprehensive cover. If you have an accident, the insurer will write off the car, giving you just the 'market value' less your excess, which means you might end up with almost nothing (and you might lose the rest of that year's premium as well). Instead go for third party only or third party fire and theft (it's not much more, see pages 86–7). If it's the other side's fault, chase for the money. If you have uninsured loss recovery insurance or legal expenses cover, you will get legal help with this.

Maintenance of an old banger will be less costly, too. At this age, you are unlikely to go to a high cost dealership franchise, so your servicing can be with lower cost garages.

The vital factor is to make sure the car has at least a few months left on its MoT when you buy. If you are not sure, ask the present owner to take it for a new MoT – offer to repay the cost if it passes.

The key point when considering finance is to know the total you will pay for the car over the life of the loan – not just the stated annual percentage rate (APR). Some dealers offer very low APRs but then build finance costs into the sticker price of the car.

❝ If you buy a car for £500, your depreciation is limited to that, and some new cars lose this much every month. ❞

131

Car dealers offer two main finance options – hire purchase (HP) and personal contract purchase (PCP). PCP packages are mainly aimed at those who might otherwise have a company car. They can be expensive but they may include other features, such as maintenance contracts and breakdown roadside rescue.

Hire purchase

Hire purchase is the traditional way of paying for a car from a dealer.

HP is what it says. You effectively hire the car for the credit period from a finance company and it only becomes legally yours after that. With other forms of credit, such as a loan or credit card, the goods you buy belong to you straight away.

You have to put down a deposit at the outset – typically 10 per cent but sometimes less when dealers run 'special offers'. Then you pay each month over anything from one to five years, but often two or three years.

At the end of the hire period, you may be required to purchase the car with a fee – this is usually a token amount but always check what this will be before you sign. With a conditional sale agreement, there is no extra fee at the end.

You cannot normally renegotiate an HP deal, so be sure you can afford the payments. Dealers may try to sell you payment protection insurance. This is rarely, if ever, worthwhile. Some dealers may also pitch 'guaranteed asset protection' (GAP insurance) – this covers you against any shortfall on your motor insurance if the car is stolen or written off. This may not be worthwhile either if it is included in your own car cover.

What about 0 per cent finance?

Zero per cent finance is where there is no interest to pay. So if the price of the car is £10,000, all you will pay over the repayment period is a total of £10,000. This sounds attractive. But it will usually be offered as an alternative to a discount or accessory upgrade. You'll probably need to put down a large deposit (30 per cent or more) and if you miss a payment or are late, you may find the whole deal (including the months you have already paid) reverts to a very high interest rate. This can be offered as hire purchase or as a personal loan.

❝ Zero per cent finance is usually offered in place of a discount. ❞

 You can check if a car you're offered is still subject to HP – or stolen – by going to www.hpicheck.com.

The pros and cons of an HP agreement

Pros

- You have the right to hand back the car if you have paid 50 per cent, but this can't happen if you are in arrears.
- You have some protection against dodgy dealers. If a statement is made about the car you have purchased or the finance deal that is false, you may be entitled to end the HP agreement and/or win compensation from the HP company itself under Section 56 of the Consumer Credit Act 1974.
- One advantage of HP over a bank loan for some people is that credit checks may be less stringent because the HP company has more hold over the vehicle and can repossess it (at least in the earlier stages of the loan) while a bank will have little recourse against a delinquent borrower.
- The dealer earns commission on selling an HP deal, so if you go the HP route, ask for a lower price. Some dealers find it easier to offer upgrades such as better radios or satnavs instead of a price cut.

Cons

- You are not the legal owner until you have paid back all the money you owe – so you can't modify the car without the finance company's permission.
- You will have to pay for any damage other than general wear and tear if you hand back the car before you have paid off all the instalments.
- You can't sell without the finance company's say-so – there is a record of cars subject to HP agreements (see bottom of page 132).

For more about payment protection insurance and the reasons why it isn't worthwhile, see pages 97-8.

Borrowing from a bank

Banks rarely offer special car deals these days (and even if they do, they really will be remarkably similar to other loans).

So instead of applying for a loan specifically for a car, you have to apply for a personal loan, which will involve a credit check (see pages 56–9).

The pros and cons of borrowing from a bank

Pros

- It may be cheaper than HP.
- You do not have to find a deposit.
- There is no final payment.
- You can borrow exactly what you need – so if you have half the money in cash from your savings, you only ask for what you want. Alternatively, you could borrow more and use the extra money for something else.
- The car is yours from the start – you do not have to ask to modify it or sell it – and if it is involved in a crash or it is written off, you are in exactly the same position as if you were a cash purchaser.
- You have more freedom to shop around car dealers if you have cash – you can buy wherever you like, including online car sellers who may often be cheaper.
- The car cannot be repossessed if you default on payments, although your bank could still pursue you for defaulting on payments.
- You may be able to renegotiate terms if you have financial difficulties.
- Interest rates are competitive.
- Loans can be flexible – you can generally repay them more quickly without penalties.

Cons

- The bank may try to sell you payment protection insurance. Which? describes this as a 'protection racket'.
- If the car turns out to be faulty, you do not have Section 75 Consumer Credit Act protection unless the loan is specifically tied to the motor purchase.
- Banks may decide you have too much borrowing already and turn you down – so always approach your bank or other lender first as you may be acceptable for HP even if turned down by a bank.

Personal contract purchase

This is only available with new cars and is mainly suitable for buyers who are prepared to accept the high costs of having a new car every two to three years. It is aimed at those who might, in the past, have been recipients of the company car perk. Taxation changes mean the company car is now only good value for a limited number of people, so some employers no longer offer this but have boosted pay packets instead.

Here you pay a deposit – typically 10 per cent – and then pay monthly instalments at a lower rate than either HP or a bank loan, usually for 24 or 36 months. At the end of that period, you have the choice of either making a substantial payment to keep the car – often 33–40 per cent of the car's purchase price – or handing the car back to the dealer and walking away.

 It's all too easy to add the cost of a car to your mortgage if you remortgage. The interest rate will almost certainly be lower. But you could find yourself paying for it over the next 20 or 25 years - well after the car will probably have been scrapped. For more information, see page 75.

If you opt for the walk-away choice, you will have to pay extra if you go over the pre-agreed mileage or if the car is damaged (because these will cut the car's value in the second-hand market).

The advantage of the walk-away option is that you don't have to worry about part-exchanging or selling and part of the finance cost is taken up by the loss you would incur anyway on depreciation. For instance, in round figure terms using the table below, the personal contract purchase total payments on a £20,600

Comparing car finance

Which? Money (2007) compared three different methods of car finance. This is what it found on a car with a £20,607 retail price bought over three years.

	Hire purchase	Bank loan	Personal contract
APR	8.9%	6.5%	10.3%
10 per cent deposit	£2,235	£0	£2,235
36 payments	£579	£631.58	£399
Optional final payment	£0	£0	£8,350
Total payable	£23,154*	£22,737	£24,624**

* The hire purchase total is based on: deposit, 36 payments and fees (£75)
** The personal contract total is based on: deposit, 35 payments and fees (£74.50)

car are about £16,300. Over three years, many cars lose up to half their original cost so the second-hand value on this car might be no more than £10,300. In that case, the driver has had the use of a car for three years at £2,000 a year.

Personal leasing

This is also aimed at the 'company car' person. There are a variety of deals available, usually for two or three years, where you pay a monthly sum, which can include some or all of servicing, roadside rescue cover, repairs, insurance, road tax – almost everything except for the fuel. At the end of the period, you give the car back and take out a new lease plan. You never own the car, nor do you have the option to buy it. This is expensive but hassle-free.

Credit cards

You might be able to buy a lower cost car with your plastic, especially if you have a 0 per cent or other low-cost interest deal. But many car dealers will hit you with a surcharge of up to 3 per cent on credit card purchases. Also, buying a car could leave you with very little credit for smaller items.

￼ Around 30,000 people in the UK are members of car-sharing clubs. ￼

CAR SHARING

You can reduce your car costs with a formal or informal car-sharing scheme.

If you don't need a car all the time – and many people can live without one full time – you can save on the average, according to the AA, £5,500 annual cost of a car by sharing one with a few or many other people.

Around 30,000 people in the UK are in car clubs where, for a small annual membership fee (often £50), they can arrange via a website or call centre to hire a self-drive car for which they are usually charged by the mile – sometimes by a set fee per hour or a mix of the two. A typical rate is £5 an hour plus 20p a mile.

You access the car with a swipe card and then input a code number into a keypad, which allows you to get the key and drive away. The costs are debited directly to your credit card. This pay-as-you-go method tends to reduce mileage as you become more careful because you can see the costs ticking up on some of the cars – much like a taxi meter.

Or you could get together with one or more friends and set up an informal car share arrangement. As long as all the drivers are insured for the vehicle, there are no other formalities. How you sort out the costs is up to you. One frequent pattern is for one user to have it weekdays and the other weekends.

The two biggest car-sharing companies are City Car Club (www.CityCarClub.co.uk) and Streetcar (www.streetcar.co.uk). A charity called Carplus (www.carplus.org.uk) has also been set up to find commercial or community-run car clubs in your area.

Home improvement

Everyone has their favourite story of the double glazing salesperson who spent so long at their house that they offered him or her blankets for the night! Home improvements are an area where it is easy to waste money – no two projects are ever exactly the same so you can't go online to compare prices against the high street.

MONEY SAVING TACTICS

Money savers must always be aware of the following points.

Decide if you really need the work to be done

Perhaps you just need a few repairs and a paint job. You can pay the earth for home improvements although you may not really need them. But it is the job of the home improvement salesperson to convince you that your life will be awful without the works. In many cases, however, a less than drastic makeover may be all you need. Your kitchen could become far better with just a new stove and some minor carpentry work while a bathroom may just require new taps and a better-tiled splashback. By keeping what you have, you might save thousands by not spending.

 Never deal with home improvement builders who turn up on your doorstep unannounced. You do have cancellation rights because they are 'doorstep sellers', but they may just walk off with your money or, if they turn up, do a shoddy job with poor materials. These rights are of little use if you cannot find the builders again or if they refuse to refund you or rectify the work.

Consider whether the work will add to the value of your property

If you intend staying in your present property for years, then the effect of anything you do on the resale value is not important. But if you intend moving soon, then you may not get back the full cost of what you are installing. The £10,000 kitchen may only add a few thousands to the worth of your home if a prospective buyer does not like your taste – think of the 1970s' passion for avocado-coloured bathrooms. You might do better doing nothing and telling a buyer that you are prepared to cut the price to reflect the fact that the kitchen or bathroom or windows need replacing.

Research from Which? among estate agency firms in 2007 show that the following jobs are those that add the most value to your home:

- Building an extension/loft conversion (equal ranking)
- Adding a bedroom
- Creating off-street parking
- Fitting a new kitchen
- Installing a new bathroom
- Building a conservatory
- Installing new central heating
- Replacing doors and windows/fitting double glazing
- Improving the flooring/improving the roofing (equal ranking)
- General decorating and painting.

Be clear in specifying the work to be done

Always get a clear idea of what you want before calling in anyone for an estimate. Most DIY outlets have a good range of home improvement items, including kitchens and bathrooms – often conservatories as well, so you can look at these in an unhurried way. You may also be able to find 'planners' either in store on online so you can measure up your rooms to see what is possible beforehand. The salesperson may have some good ideas, but if you just let him or her have a free run, you'll end up paying much more than you should. Pick up leaflets and look at magazines for ideas as well.

Work out how you will pay for the improvements

Always start off by deciding how much you can afford to pay and then stick to this. Look at the options you have for raising cash – remember that the credit deal the home improvement person tries to sell may be among the most expensive. The company will earn a further commission if they sell you a loan. In some cases, this commission on the credit may be so large that sellers will offer a discount on the improvements themselves if you take up their loan.

Consider the implications of moving versus improving

There is a time when a growing family needs more space. The choice may be between moving somewhere larger or staying where you are and extending upwards into the loft space, sideways into a garage, outwards into the back garden or even downwards to bring a cellar back into use as living space. Some people now even dig under their house in order to create a new basement (but this is very expensive).

 For more information on your options for raising cash, see pages 54–76.

If you dislike your present home, there is probably no contest. But if you like the area, the neighbours, the transport, the schools, the shops, then improving can be worthwhile. Remember that in many areas moving can cost £25,000 or more in estate agency fees, stamp duty, mortgage fee, legal costs and removal expenses (and that's not counting the trauma and time involved in moving home). This will go a long way towards many extensions or other improvement projects.

❝ The £25,000 cost of moving home will go a long way towards many extensions or other improvement projects. ❞

Beware of over-improvement

This is where you spend so much on the home, that it becomes too expensive for the neighbourhood. Someone with a £100,000 terraced house buying a £50,000 kitchen would be in this category. There is simply no way that expense would ever be recouped in a sale. It could even put off a prospective purchaser. Of course, if you don't intend moving, you can do what you like – but this is not saving money.

DEALING WITH SALES PEOPLE

Here are some of the tricks of the sales trade. Some are very old but that does not stop them being effective – they are used because they work. They are worth looking at in some detail because failing to spot them can literally mean the difference between spending and saving thousands of pounds.

Most home-improvement sellers are paid mainly (sometimes wholly) by commission. This is usually 10 per cent of the contract price, rising to 20 per cent in some companies. The seller's managers may also receive a commission if the seller hits a target – known as a

You have no legal right to the statutory seven-day cooling-off period if you sign a contract in your home (as opposed to on trade premises) provided the seller did not arrive on your doorstep unannounced. Sellers generally make sure they are 'invited' into your home by arranging an appointment first with you. So you only have one chance of avoiding an expensive mistake – not signing. In theory, if they call you and arrange an appointment, you have the legal cooling-off period protection. But many home improvement companies get around this by first arranging a non-sales meeting, where you will be invited to make an appointment. And if they leave a card and then you call them, you lose your cancellation rights.

'volume override' – so the end result is a substantial slice of your money in their bank accounts. But if they don't get your agreement to the contract on offer, their standard of living falls back to a minimal level, so they will try all manner of ways to get that vital signature.

The discount technique

This is the most basic technique in the seller's armoury – convincing you that you have a bargain. It can be very easy because home improvements are individual and few people have any idea as to what they should cost. These are not known-value items where most people have a good idea of price, such as tins of baked beans or highly advertised competitive items such as basic computers.

According to industry sources, the typical gross margin in home improvements is 40 per cent. That means that of every £1,000 you pay, £600 goes towards materials and the specialised labour needed to fit them while £400 pays for the company, its marketing, the commission it pays, its premises and all the other costs a business incurs.

So when you are told there is a 50 per cent discount 'special offer', be very suspicious. The figures do not add up. If you took 50 per cent from the £1,000, you would get £500, which would mean the company either had to do your work at a loss (as it needs £600 for materials) or that it is lying about the cost. It could occasionally mean that the company is so badly run that it is about to go out of business – taking your money with it. The discount price is where you start to haggle – there are tips on haggling on pages 128–9.

Variations on the discount include 'buy seven windows and we'll give you two doors for free', and 'get a kitchen from us and you'll get a free stove/television/dishwasher'.

The 'seven windows of any size for £1,400' technique

This sounds like a money saver. It is not. Firms that advertise this seeming bargain may forget to tell you that while that's what you pay for the windows, you'll pay extra for almost everything else, such as removal of your old windows, the labour in fitting the new ones – and you could find yourself paying extra for the handles and the locks as well – often a lot extra.

The flattery technique

You'll be told that because the firm is new in the area, it would like to advertise itself by using your home as a show place. You'll be flattered and impressed because you will get a discount. In fact, you will end up paying just the same as you would otherwise. The firm may not

❝ Be very suspicious of a 50 per cent 'special offer' discount as the figures just won't add up. ❞

be new to the area, anyway – it doesn't matter as long as you sign.

A variation on this is the brochure or magazine. Property owners think *House Beautiful* or even *Hello!*, but all that happens, if anything, is that the seller takes a polaroid picture and it ends up in a loose-leaf binder. This may also be used to get an initial foot in the door – cold-calling kitchen sellers will tell you that you will get a discount because your property will appear in a magazine.

The 'I'll call my manager' technique

As the clock approaches midnight and the seller is aware you are likely to fall asleep, he'll say that because it is the end of his month (never true) and he needs just one more sale to pass his bonus level/keep his job (depending on how he finds you), then he'll call his manager to see if he can't cut the price back again.

It is highly unlikely that the manager will be taking calls at this time (or any other), but the seller will call someone – perhaps the speaking clock or a fellow salesman elsewhere – and have a heated conversation, which will remarkable result in the triumphant declaration that the manager has said that the job has been overpriced and that the asking price should be cut at once.

The 'drop close' technique

This is where the price apparently 'drops' so the seller can 'close' the deal with your signature. You'll be told that if you do not sign there and then, the price will go up the next day. Ignore this. The drop price is the one you could start to haggle on the next day. Sellers are trained to be thick-skinned and ignore setbacks such as you saying no – so don't have too many concerns about their feelings as they will probably have none for yours.

> **Sales techniques include flattery, a fake call to a manager, and the drop price that is a discount with a deadline attached.**

The 'subject to survey' technique

This is very sneaky. You'll be asked to sign a contract with a price that you feel comfortable with. But it will be late at night and you do not read the small print that says you've agreed that the price is 'subject to survey'. A week or two later, after you've cancelled other salespeople, the 'surveyor' turns up and discovers that there are many hidden problems that were not costed into the job in the first place. So you'll have to pay more. Fortunately, they cannot force you to pay the higher price and if the terms and conditions said you had to accept the higher price, you can still challenge the term as being unfair. Show the surveyor and his company the door.

The 'new company' technique

You were quoted £5,000 for your windows, which you thought was too much. The seller knows that there is a reasonable profit if the windows were £3,000. So a week or two after the rejection, you get a call either from the same salesperson saying he has moved to another firm and the price is now £4,000 or you get the same offer from another firm (which has bought your details from the seller who visited you). An alternative is that you are phoned by the 'commercial' department of the company, which will explain that it normally only carries out big contracts on office blocks or shopping centres, but it just happens to have some spare capacity so it offers you a special deal at the lower prices it charges to big building contracts.

❝ Get a fixed price: an estimate is worthless, and make sure there are dates and penalty clauses in the contract and that everything is itemised. ❞

GET A PROPER CONTRACT

You can save a lot of money if you have a proper contract for your home improvement. There is a variety of contracts, but the most useful for consumers for small building works is the 'JCT Building Contract for a home owner/occupier who has not appointed a consultant to oversee the work'.

Good contract practice

- **Make sure you have a fixed price** – an estimate is worthless.
- **Ensure you have dates in the contract** for finishing each stage of the job (if the size of the job merits this) or the job itself (some contracts allow for severe weather delays on outdoor jobs). A competent contractor will have no problem with this.
- **Include penalty clauses** for time overruns, which could save you money because it can be costly to have builders for too long in your home. These are really only applicable on more sizeable jobs.
- **Itemise everything** and include an agreement that they will let you know extra charges and will ask you for permission beforehand.
- **Never give a builder money upfront,** even for 'materials' (although if it is a small job, there is no harm in providing the materials yourself to the builder's

 To find out more about the Joint Contracts Tribunal (JCT) and the different types of contract that are available, go to www.jctltd.co.uk. See also the *Which? Essential Guide Develop Your Property.*

specification). Your contract should be payment in arrears with percentages at each stage of the job if it is going to continue for a good few months.

- **Keep back 10–15 per cent as a 'retention'**, payable in six months' time if all the 'snags' – those annoying little faults that often appear in the best of jobs – have been sorted. The retention will enable you to hire someone else if the builder defaults.
- **Try not to add to the job** once it has started. If you really feel there is extra work to do, always get a quotation from your supplier before the work is done.

It can be worthwhile paying more to a builder who is professional enough to agree to a proper contract than to give cash to a cowboy.

> **❝ The NRWAS is a 'home improvement broker' who could protect you from high-pressure selling. ❞**

A different way of getting quotes

As a basic rule, never consider any home improvement until you have seen at least three firms and received three binding quotations. But it could also be worth looking at the National Replacement Window Advisory Service (NRWAS), which also includes the National Home Improvement Advisory Service and the National Conservatory Advisory Service (see box below).

The NRWAS is a 'home improvement broker', which can spare you the trouble of seeing a large number of firms and save you from dealing with the potential of a high-pressure selling session.

If you use it, the adviser will first discuss your needs on the phone. If you go further, someone will be sent to your home to look at the work required. Your details are then faxed to a number of home improvement firms, which then send back quotations. It chooses the best quotation for you and recommends this. You are under no obligation to accept this. If you do, the company that wins your contract pays NRWAS a fixed fee (not a commission based on a percentage of the work value).

Companies know that paying the NRWAS fee is less than employing a commission-based salesperson so they can tender more competitively for work.

The National Replacement Window Advisory Service (NRWAS), National Home Improvement Advisory Service and the National Conservatory Advisory Service are all on www.nrwas.org or phone 0870 7706606.

For instance, on a window replacement job, the NRWAS fee might be £250. But assuming a salesperson quotes £10,000, the window company knows it will probably have to pay £1,000 (often more) to the seller. So it can reduce the quote by the difference – £750 – to be competitive and still earn as much. You have saved £750 plus not had to deal with several sellers who might subject you to a hard sell.

If you contact the NRWAS, your address (other than nearest town or postal district in a big city) and phone number are kept secret from any of the companies it contacts.

Money saving tip

Getting involved in your own kitchen and bathroom makeover rather than leaving it all to a home improvement company should pay dividends. Sourcing the sink, cooker, furniture and bathroom suite at a do-it-yourself superstore and then finding an installer locally will generally be cheaper. You will also have much more control over the job as you can hire and fire workers rather than having to accept those you are given.

" By using the NRWAS, you save paying hidden sales commission and do not have to deal with the hard sell from several different sellers. "

Down at the furniture store

Furniture is one of the biggest ticket items on the high street. It is also one of the most problematic as so much is made for the individual customer that it is almost impossible to compare specifications in the way you might with a computer.

There is very little furniture sold on the internet and almost zero brand recognition so there are no best-buy lists. And there is a wide variety of prices for goods that perform the same function – you could buy a dining table and four chairs for £20 at a junk or charity shop or for £2,000 at an upmarket store.

Money savers can often find bargains (or goods for free) on websites such as freecycle (www.freecycle.org) or www.ecyclebin.com where people give away furniture and other items that they no longer want. This can include tables, chairs, cupboards, bookcases and office furniture. Also try www.gumtree.com – it's a site where individuals can put up adverts for items they wish to sell for free.

Beyond that, you probably pay for what you get. But unless you intend your furniture to outlast you, there is little point in going to the more expensive stores. A cheap £200 sofa will last a few years – so if that's all you are likely to want before moving on, there is no point in spending ten times that much.

Some furniture stores offer both free credit and 'nothing to pay for a year'. The cost of the credit is, of course, built in to the price, so if you don't need credit, you could find better deals elsewhere. If you do find the offer attractive, don't forget that if you default on a payment or are late by even one day, some agreements automatically revert to a very high interest rate – and you may be charged interest as well on the 'free period'. Always check on the small print – and never buy payment protection insurance.

Money saving tip

December is a good time to buy furniture and carpets when stores are empty and staff ready to cut a deal.

 For more information about loans, see pages 54–76. The inside story on payment protection insurance is given on page 98.

ALWAYS TRY TO PAY BY CREDIT CARD

Furniture companies can and do go bust, although these company collapses rarely make headlines. If this happens, buyers who have paid deposits or all the purchase price become 'unsecured creditors', which really means you are bottom of the heap when it comes to paying out any money that is still in the company's coffers or can be raised by selling its assets.

Besides checking to see if there is adverse comment on any website before buying, the most obvious way of ensuring you don't hand over your money to a bust furniture company is to pay by credit card (not debit card or cheque or cash), so you get the protection of the Consumer Credit Act, 1974 (see page 63). This can be a deposit only but as long as the goods are worth over £100 (and almost all furniture purchases will be), you are covered against dealer default.

Ignore 'VAT-free' or 'VAT-paid'

There is no such thing as 'we pay the VAT' or 'VAT-free' on furniture sales. Whatever you pay, the store has to divide the amount by 117.5 and multiply the result by 17.5 and then hand that over to the tax authorities. It's trying to convince you of a saving that may or may not be useful to you – but it is certainly not paying the VAT. Money savers just look at how much they will pay. It's the pounds that count – not how they might arrive at the sum.

This 'sleight of hand' is also common on home improvement adverts.

“ The obvious way to protect your money is to pay by credit card so you are covered by the Consumer Credit Act. ”

The daily shop

Love them or loathe them, supermarkets are part
and parcel of shopping today. But knowing a few of
their tricks will help you save money – and cut back
on waste. This chapter shows you how. It also tells
you when buying in bulk can be a good or a bad idea
and it helps you pay less for non-food items as well.

Supermarket tricks

Most supermarket groups say they are the best value around. But unless you have all day to spare and don't pay for transport, it's not worth spending pounds in travel and time to save pennies by going around several supermarkets for individual items. However, if you are making a big food purchase, it can really be worth shopping around.

REDUCING YOUR WEEKLY SPEND

Here are some ideas to help reduce your weekly spend.

Buy fresh food from other sources

These goods generally make more profit for supermarkets than packaged goods. Meat, fish, fruit and vegetables can often be cheaper at butchers, fishmongers or greengrocers. Street markets can often offer fresh food bargains, especially mid-afternoon when they are usually packing up for the day and don't want to take items away unsold that may not be so sellable the next day.

Mid-afternoon bargain hunters may need to buy more groceries than they would normally do – so money savers need to work out recipes that can use a lot of one item or use freezers or other storage.

Sign up for a loyalty card if you are a regular

Supermarkets monitor your spending and send you vouchers either to encourage you to buy items on your regular list or to try new ideas. One trick is to sign up to a card, spend a reasonable amount at the supermarket every week or more often for a few weeks and then go elsewhere for your shopping. You may then get vouchers offering big discounts off your weekly shop to attract you back. For instance, Tesco may send a £7-off voucher if you spend £50 or more to customers it has not seen for some time.

The loyalty cards offered by Sainsbury'a, Tesco and Homebase are a bonus if you intend to go shopping in these stores, but they are not a primary reason to go there. They are generally worth 1p in the pound and, as these are often paid in the form of vouchers that

 The Office of Fair Trading (OFT) is responsible for making markets work well for consumers, so if you have any complaints, go to the OFT website at www.oft.gov.uk.

are only usable in the particular chain of stores, you have to go back there and shop again. Tesco vouchers can sometimes be used to buy leisure tickets such as admission to theme parks and other attractions, which are particularly good value.

No supermarket group is ever the cheapest for everything. They will tend to compete on 'known value items' such as milk or bread, which only make up a small proportion of your total spend. Supermarkets know the products where most customers are aware of prices. So while supermarkets may be cheaper for white sliced bread, if you prefer less heavily sold items, such as wholemeal or rye bread, these could be more expensive to purchase.

Never assume that a supermarket chain has the same prices in all its stores

Some groups now have a hierarchy of stores – very large, large, convenience, upmarket location, petrol station and motorway service stations – and prices could be different at each. There can be regional differences as well and the goods are changed from one area to the next, with more expensive brands in the better-off neighbourhoods. If you want, for instance, a basic honey for cooking a cake, you may not find it in an affluent area where you will only be offered a variety of better, but pricier, honeys.

Some stores also use 'dynamic pricing' so items can be cheaper at less popular shopping times such as Monday afternoon than Saturday morning.

Look for special offers

Bogofs or 'buy one get one free' are popular as is the variation 'buy two and get 50p or £1 off'. But it's the price you pay per item rather than the sticker price that counts. Supermarkets have been accused of raising prices dramatically on items one week (and being happy to sell very little) only to reduce them just as substantially the next so they can claim a 'discount' or 'bogof'. One of the problems of this form of marketing is that it often assumes people buy items in twos – not so good if you are living alone. One supermarket sold mangoes at £1.20 with a bogof, so you got two for £1.20 or 60p each. The local greengrocer sold the same fruit at 55p each.

The daily shop

Money saving tip

Don't get caught buying fancy named painkillers. Many over the counter (non-prescription) drugs come in two versions – branded and often high cost and generic. Nurofen is a major brand name of generic drug ibuprofen. The active ingredient is the same but Nurofen can cost twice as much as non-branded ibuprofen. Nurofen gel for muscular pains, strains and sprains is more expensive than generic versions such as 'Deep Relief'. There is also a big price gap between branded Panadol and generic paracetamol. Your pharmacist will advise you.

Always look at the unit price

Big packages are not always cheaper than small ones. Remember that 50p-off per kilo is not very much if the item is light and bought by the 100g-size pack when the reduction is equal to just 5p per packet.

Buy lower cost items as they arise

Stock up on lower cost items (or at least those with a long shelf life) when you see them. These deals are often partly paid for by food (and other) manufacturers as promotions. They can't afford to subsidise their sale to the supermarkets at these very low prices for very long so grab them while they are on offer.

Take vouchers for sports equipment or computers for schools when offered. And make sure you hand them in to your local educational establishment. But don't make them a prime reason to shop in a store – they are only worth a fraction of a penny for each pound you spend.

> ## Money saving tip
>
> **Taking cash to a supermarket instead of relying on a credit or debit card can reduce your propensity to overspend.**

Use budget supermarkets

The UK has three major chains – Lidl, Aldi and Netto – which are consistently cheaper on many items than the major supermarket. Some shoppers say that there are amazing bargains to be found, especially in wine, chocolate, German sausages (Lidl and Aldi are German while Netto is Danish) and cleaning materials, such as detergent. But others report cats and dogs refusing to eat the pet food. They can offer lower prices as there are no free plastic bags and they don't take credit cards (where the bank takes a cut). And they don't 'look good' or offer home delivery. If you find items you like there, there are some savings to be made.

> ## Money saving tip
>
> **Look out for seasonal bargains. The best time to buy a bike is in October after the summer selling season is over and before the year's new designs (often little more than a fresh paint colour job) come in for Christmas. Many retailers slash 20 per cent from list prices – or £80 on a mid-price bike.**

❝Reduced prices are often subsidised by manufacturers, so they won't last for long. ❞

WHAT ABOUT OWN BRAND?

Own-label goods are usually cheaper than well-known brands, but are they the same? Some are made in the same factory to the same recipe. Others may be manufactured to a cheaper formula. It often depends on how basic a food is. There may be no point in paying more for a branded pasta or rice where any difference is likely to be indiscernible, but many people say branded breakfast cereals taste better.

A tin of own-brand plum tomatoes may cost 25p against 45p for a well-known brand. What's the difference? The cheaper one will have smaller or more mis-shaped tomatoes. If you are using the tomatoes in a recipe, who will notice?

But take more care with the very low-cost 'value' or 'white label' or 'economy' items. These can sometimes be low quality. Cheap soup may be largely water, colouring and flavour thickened with flour while some budget washing-up liquids require you to use a lot more than a premium brand to achieve the same amount of cleaning. So these economy brands can sometimes be a false economy.

66 Money savers have a list and stick to it to avoid unnecessary buys. 99

GETTING YOU TO BUY MORE

Supermarkets want you to fill up those large trolleys with impulse buys. But a large amount of what people buy goes to waste because they purchase more than they can eat or buy books or CDs they will never read or listen to. One estimate says we throw away a third of the food that we buy. While some of that is inedible items, such as egg shells and banana skins, much of it is good food. Money savers always shop with a list and keep to it.

Supermarkets are also good at getting you to stay longer than you might otherwise have done through providing a restaurant and free newspapers. The café will usually be before the checkout, so you can relax before spending more.

Supermarkets are expert in getting you to spend more than you planned. Almost everyone knows that tempting impulse items known as 'eye candy' are often put next to the checkout where you have to wait. But because everyone is so aware of this, some stores now use this space to advertise their phone and financial services offers instead. The 'eye candy' is now often more subtly positioned.

- **The 'triangulation' trick.** Supermarkets work out the level where your eye naturally looks and put items with the highest profit margin there. Items

 Check out prices of expensive items on the supermarkets' websites before you shop. Similarly, pricing your shopping list from an online source is helpful if your money is tight.

placed lower on the shelves are often cheaper, as are those that only a tall person can reach!

- **The 'moving items around' trick.** Moving tea from aisle 3 to aisle 13 confuses you and ensures you spend more time in store and pass more items that might tempt you.
- **End-aisle items** where you slow down with your trolley to turn are also particularly good places for displaying higher-profit items.
- **The most expensive goods,** such as electricals, are placed by the entrance and the most basic foods, such as meat and milk, near the exit so you have to go past the alluring computers and hi-fi before you get to the bread and butter.
- **Bread and coffee** are often located at the back of the store, so that the pleasant smells wafting down the aisles attract you to walk the whole depth as well as length of the shop.

&&Expensive goods are placed by the entrance and basic items are near the exit. ,,

Buying online

You can save a lot of money buying goods ranging from books to computers online. But always look out for hidden extras, such as carriage costs and postage charges for returning goods.

COMPARISON SITES

Research funded by the Economic and Social Research Council (ESRC) in 2006 showed that consumers can reap bigger than expected benefits from shopping online as internet retailers change prices more frequently than traditional stores and are more likely to cut them than to increase them.

Goods that are ideally suited to internet shopping are those that are high cost but easy to transport, such as cameras and computers. Specialised parts and components are also much easier to find online.

To save time, there are a number of price-comparison sites, which mostly show prices including all delivery charges and taxes (where applicable) so you can compare fairly. No site has everything – online retailers have to sign contracts with the price sites, which not all are willing to do – but the great majority are on at least one site.

But don't choose just by price for you could end up dealing with a retailer who is outside the UK and whose reliability is unknown. For instance, some people purchasing games consoles, which sold at £400 in the UK from an online site offering them at £350, discovered the machines only worked in the Far East. This retailer, who mainly dealt with the Far East, said it never promised a machine that would work in the UK. In any case, it was outside of UK consumer law and so there were no refunds.

Sites are more likely to be competitive when there are a large number of competing retailers selling an item. No one wants to be at the bottom of a list where the top is the least expensive. The order that firms appear in can change daily – as do prices – so if you see something attractive, you will not necessarily save money by waiting.

Some retailers, such as PC World and Argos, offer a store pick-up service.

 The main sites for general shopping are www.checkaprice.com, www.kelkoo.co.uk, www.pricegrabber.co.uk, www.pricerunner.co.uk and www.shopping.com.

You order online and collect at the shop where you pay. The advantage is that you don't pay for carriage, you don't pay in advance (so you don't need a credit card) and you pick up the items when you want (within a time frame) rather than having to wait for delivery at home. Furthermore, you are also dealing with a known retailer.

HOME DELIVERY

There are some items, such as furniture or large fridges, that you simply cannot collect yourself – unless you have or hire a huge van; and then you really should pay attention to health and safety when you lift these items. Some stores charge extra for this, but enough stores that sell large items offer free delivery (such as John Lewis), so you should be able to avoid this extra expense. Home delivery is also useful for smaller items as it can save on fares, parking, petrol and your time. Again, it may be free.

But the biggest growth area in home delivery is food. Many supermarkets will deliver what you have chosen online to your home, often specifying a one-hour delivery slot. They generally charge £5 for this – a bargain for many people as it saves a visit to the supermarket (and this never seems to take less than an hour). You don't need a car either. There are, however, disadvantages.

- You're buying blind – you don't get to prod the produce before you buy.
- If something is not in stock, you may not be happy with any replacement the store sends you.

At least when you shop in person you can always look for new ideas as well.

SPECIAL DEALS

Many retailers regularly send customers emails with details of special offers, which can include everything from free carriage to free upgrades on electronics to free boxes of chocolates. They would rather more people see this, so many of these giveaways are listed on www.hotukdeals.com/vouchers, so it's worth checking to see if you can cut the cost of online purchasing. Of course, you should only deal with retailers you know

 More specialist book, music and DVD sites include www.123pricecheck.com and www.find-dvd.co.uk, while www.shopgenie.co.uk specialises in electronics.

Know your online rights

Shopping online (or by mail order) can be convenient – and sometimes also cheaper than the high street – but it can be easy to make a mistake when placing an order through a website.

You may have to rely on a photo and description on a website rather than seeing the item in the flesh. So anyone buying online (or by mail order or over the phone or fax) gets the additional protection of the Consumer Protection (Distance Selling) Regulations, 2000.

What you can do

- Which? Legal Services says the Consumer Protection Regulations gives a 'cooling-off' period, when you can change your mind and cancel an order. When you buy goods you have seven working days, starting from the day after you receive them, to cancel and you do not have to give a reason for cancelling the order.

- If you are buying a service (for example, upgrading your mobile phone contract), the cooling-off period starts the day after you place your order.

- Anyone buying insurance online or over the phone has a 14-day cancellation period.

- If you are outside the cooling-off period, check the seller's terms and conditions – some companies give you longer (as much as 28 days) to return things you don't want.

- The seller's terms and conditions should also say who pays for returning goods; if it's not made clear, then the seller has to pay.

- The terms and conditions may also specify a particular way of returning goods, but these must be reasonable – the seller can't have a procedure that is so expensive or involved that it would be cheaper and easier to keep the goods.

What you can't do

- There are some items that you can't return:
  - CDs, DVDs or software if you've broken the seal on the wrapping.
  - Perishable items, such as food and flowers.
  - Tailor-made or personalised goods, such as engraved trophies or monogrammed items.

- If you have agreed that a service will start straight away (for example, car breakdown cover), you give up your cancellation rights.

and trust – after all, a 25 per cent reduction is of little use if you have no confidence in the store.

Some offers are not quite what they seem, however. For example, when wine merchant Threshers sent out millions of 40 per cent-off wine vouchers in November 2006, the offer had to be compared with the store's standard 'three bottles for two' or 33.3 per cent-off pricing. The 40 per cent discount was better (it applied to just one bottle and made it easier to calculate the prices of cases of mixed wines) but not exactly 40 per cent off the normal price – just 7 per cent or so off its permanently three-for-two reduced price if you bought wine in multiples of three bottles.

PROTECTION WHEN BUYING ONLINE

When you're ordering something through a website, it's easy to make a mistake – you might, for example, order 11 items by pressing the '1' key twice without realising it. So, under the Electronic Commerce Regulations, 2002, online retailers must:

- Set out the different stages that you have to complete to place an order.
- Give you the chance to check the details you have inputted before the order is placed.
- Give full details of who they are and both a geographical address and an email address to contact them at.
- Acknowledge your order once you've placed your order. Check carefully what the email says. If it confirms acceptance of your order, you have a legally binding contract, but if it just acknowledges receipt of your order (perhaps because the seller needs to first check whether the item you want is in stock), you don't.

❝ Some offers are not what they seem. One 40 per cent-off deal was really only worth just 7 per cent. ❞

Read the T&Cs

Always read the retailer's terms and conditions. They may, for example, say that the price of the goods you have ordered will be fixed the day they are despatched to you. This is generally bad

 If you are trying to find unusual or expensive food or drink items, try www.mysupermarket.co.uk.

because it gives you no certainty and could give the retailer a blank cheque to overcharge you. But it can be reasonable if the goods are seasonal (such as some foods) and the price is continually changing or if the goods have to come from overseas where they are priced in a foreign currency, which can fluctuate. This may mean that if the price is higher than when you placed the order, you should have the chance to cancel, otherwise you could challenge the contract terms as unfair.

If something you've bought is faulty

As well as the special rights you have when buying online or by mail order, you have rights under the Sale of Goods Act, 2003 that apply to things you buy in person. This says that items must be 'fit for the purpose', as described, and of satisfactory quality. If you have to return a faulty item, tell the supplier and give the company the chance to collect them; if it won't, ask for the cost of postage back.

As soon as you know that what you ordered isn't what you want, let the seller know. Check the seller's terms and conditions to see if they say how you should do this. If you cancel by phone, confirm it in writing (an email is fine), and make sure you do it within the cooling-off period.

Return the item as soon as you can. The seller's terms should say who must pay for sending something back – if they don't say, then they must pay (either by arranging to collect the item, or refunding the postage). The terms and conditions may also say how items must be returned, but these must be reasonable – the seller can't have requirements that are so expensive or involved that it would be cheaper and easier to keep the item. It would be unreasonable, for instance, to insist on a motorcycle courier to return a book costing £10, but it would be fair to demand more than second-class postage if the item was a £10,000 watch.

As soon as you realise there is a problem with the item, decide what you want done. If you want your money back, you have only a 'reasonable' time to 'reject' something that has a fault or problem and get your money back. As a general rule, three to four weeks is the normal return limit, but if the problem is immediately obvious, it may be less, so write to the supplier as soon as you become aware of it.

If you get no response or the seller simply refuses your request, your main options are to call on your credit card company citing Section 75 of the Consumer Credit Act, 1974 or going to the small claims court.

See page 9 for more information about the Sale of Goods Act, 2003 and page 63 for more information about the Consumer Credit Act, 1974. See also the *Which? Essential Guide Making a Civil Claim* for details about small claims courts.

BUYING FROM AUCTION SITES

This area of buying online is very much 'buyer beware' where money savings may have to be balanced against the security of dealing with a known retailer. Many items on these sites are from private sellers so you have very few rights if the goods fail to live up to their description. Always check the site's terms and conditions – you may not have any protection, for instance, if you buy concert or sports tickets at more than their face value. Paypal, the payment system owned by eBay refuses, for instance, to deal with any complaints past a 45-day cut-off period or with anyone about tickets that are 'intangible' – the seller does not have them physically, which can happen when a popular concert is sold out in minutes and then successful applicants re-offer the tickets.

Money saving tip

Always try more than one price-comparison site before buying online. Go to http://paler.com for a listing of sites you can try. This includes many that are not well publicised as well as some specialist sites for purchases ranging from computer games to vintage wine.

❝Balance money savings against the security of dealing with a known retailer. Buying privately gives you very few rights.❞

Paying customs duties

You cannot just bring anything you want freely into the country from overseas. Besides restrictions on offensive items, such as guns or pornography, and safety regulations that ban meat or toys from certain countries, your 'bargain' may not appear so cheap when HM Customs & Excise adds on duties and taxes.

BUYING ONLINE

If you buy online from a country outside the European Union, you may have to pay customs duties and/or VAT on arrival – plus a fee to the Post Office or other delivery company for collecting the money. The overseas company may not tell you about this – it would be very difficult anyway for a US company to know all about the different tax and duty schemes across the world.

Customs duty is waived if the amount of duty is less than £7 and import VAT is not payable on:

- Commercial consignments, such as goods purchased over the internet with a value not exceeding £18, but this does not include alcohol, tobacco products, perfume or toilet waters.
- Gifts, excluding alcohol, tobacco, perfumes and toilet waters, with a value not exceeding £36.

Many cut-price online DVD and CD stores will send your consignment in a number of different parcels to avoid tax as, in most cases, each item is worth less than £18.

There is no extra tax to pay when you bring in goods bought from an online store in the European Union because tax has already been paid. This does not apply to alcohol and tobacco products.

❝ Many cut-price online DVD and CD stores send goods in a number of separate parcels to avoid extra tax. ❞

 To keep up to date with customs duty, go to Her Majesty's Revenue & Customs website on www.hmrc.gov.uk.

THE BOOZE CRUISE

Going to a French channel port to buy alcohol (or to Belgium to buy tobacco) can save a lot of money. For example, it would be easy on just 90 litres of mid-priced wine (120 bottles) to save over £500 on a trip. But you can also get into trouble with HM Revenue & Customs, who can seize your shopping or even your car.

The goods you bring back have to have had duty paid on them in the country of purchase at that country's rate – so beer and wine are cheap in France while tobacco is a bargain in Belgium. But they must also be for personal consumption or use and not for resale. 'Own use' includes reasonable gifts and big occasions such as a wedding.

There is some dispute over exactly how much this means. If you were organising a very big party, you could argue you needed 200 bottles of champagne. But customs might want some proof, such as details of the wedding or other celebration.

However, most illegality takes place with tobacco, which is light, simple to transport, easy to sell and where the gap between UK prices and those in Belgium is substantial. Tobacco also has a limited shelf life so Customs will have some idea of what is reasonable for personal use.

Is it worth it?

You can generally expect to save around 30–50 per cent on the UK price of beer and wine – less on spirits – importing goods in this way. Comparisons can sometimes be difficult as the brands you might see in France may not be sold here – this is especially so for drinks such as port and sherry. In general, though, the more expensive the wine, the smaller the percentage (but the actual saving may still be very worthwhile).

Some retailers such as Majestic have an online catalogue so you can pre-order. There may be discounts if you buy more than a case (12 bottles) or half a case (6 bottles) of the same wine. A number of retailers accept UK cash or cheques in sterling and some will even give you a free ferry ticket at the least popular times of the year for travel, such as November or February.

You have to factor in the cost of your time, car fuel, any extra insurance needed to drive abroad, the ferry crossing and any meals you take. So the further you live from the Channel ports, the less you'll gain. But you can make it more

---

What could be subject to questioning?

As a rule, anyone who is importing more than 3,200 cigarettes (or 200 cigars, 400 cigarillos or 3kg of tobacco), 110 litres of beer, 90 litres of wine, 10 litres of spirits or 20 litres of fortified wine (such as port or sherry) could be subject to questioning at a channel port.

worthwhile if you combine a visit to a supermarket with a weekend or day away. But don't overload the car with bottles so it either breaks down or becomes dangerous to drive – you could invalidate part of your insurance if you knowingly make a car unstable. And that would more than wipe out your money saving trip.

There are no 'duty free' concessions within the European Union but special rules apply from some destinations, including the Channel Islands and the Canaries. You can, however, sometimes buy money saving goods at UK airport shops 'airside' – after you have been through passport control. Some airport stores advertise 'VAT-free' prices aimed at those people leaving the UK, but anyone can purchase there without customs concerns when they return.

❛❛ Don't overload your car so that it breaks down or is dangerous to drive. ❜❜

SHOPPING TRIPS OUTSIDE THE EUROPEAN UNION

The duty-free concept still applies when you return from destinations outside the EU including the Channel Islands and the Canaries. You can bring in without paying UK tax or duty:

- 200 cigarettes;
  or 100 cigarillos;
  or 50 cigars;
  or 250g of tobacco
  (not for under 17s)
- 60cc of perfume
- 2 litres of still table wine
  (not for under 17s)
- 250cc of eau de toilette
- 1 litre of spirits or strong liqueurs over 22 per cent volume;
  or 2 litres of fortified wine, sparkling wine or other liqueurs, such as port or sherry
  (not for under 17s)
- £145 worth of all other goods, including gifts and souvenirs.

The government has intended upgrading the £145 allowance for some time but this requires international co-operation.

Buying in bulk

The more you buy, the cheaper the price gets. From popcorn at the cinema to quantities of kitchen paper, going for the biggest size brings lower prices. But don't buy so much that you end up wasting most of it.

There are a number of cash and carry-style warehouses open to the public, such as Costco and Makro. They specialise in selling large packs of food and other goods but some also sell garments and shoes including 'famous brands' (often remainders from a previous season, so you might only find very small and very large sizes).

Some have an extensive range of departments, including car parts, bedding, cameras, electrical, sports products, furniture, office necessities and garden goods. But don't expect a wide range – they keep prices down by holding limited stocks of goods, sometimes from less well-known manufacturers or by only keeping a limited range or colours and sizes on clothing items.

Some quote prices excluding VAT but most now show them both including and excluding VAT. There is no VAT on fresh foods and no tax on some packaged foods.

These stores are primarily aimed at small business needs. But you are not limited to goods that are applicable to your business – a substantial part of these stores is devoted to packaged and fresh food, which you can buy if your business is, for instance, repairing cars.

MONEY SAVING STARTS WITH MONEY SPENDING

You generally have to join, paying a membership of around £25 a year. Most of these stores limit membership to those with a business – producing a VAT number or a business letterhead is a requirement. But members can pay for cards for others, such as staff or friends, so it is relatively easy to join.

Additionally, some allow 'guests' to accompany cardholders. The guests cannot buy at the checkout but there is nothing to stop the host paying in cash and the guest giving the money as soon as the goods are bought.

IS IT WORTH IT?

Yes, provided you do not have to travel too far, you can deal with very large packs of some items and you are not too fussed about brands on more individual goods. There are some very low prices – even when the VAT is added back in. But if you do not want the very large sizes, many prices may be just as competitive in lower cost supermarkets.

But the best way to find out is ask someone with a card to take you first as a guest to check out what you can make a saving on.

Taxing matters

You can pay less in tax – legally. This chapter shows how to reduce the tax inspector's take without employing a high-cost accountant. Find out how to avoid paying penalties and interest payments by keeping to a few simple rules, whether you work for someone else, work for yourself or a mixture of both.

Checking your tax bill

There are some 30 million taxpayers in the UK. Mistakes are made both by employers who deduct tax and by the tax office. Understanding and questioning your tax code could save you cash.

There are a number of tax code letters. Together with the number (such as 512L), they tell the employer how much of your income is tax-free and how much tax to deduct. But costly mistakes can occur, especially if you have more than one job or change employment. The main tax code letters are defined in the box below. If you have overpaid, you will be due a rebate from Her Majesty's Revenue & Customs (HMRC). But if you have underpaid, you might have to pay interest on the amount due.

Ask your employer why you have the code you have or contact the tax office that deals with your employer.

INVESTING IN YOUR FIRM

There are a number of tax-saving schemes that enable you to buy a stake in your employer's firm if it has shares. Many are complex and need specialist advice, but the simplest and most widespread is Save As You Earn (SAYE), which combines tax benefits with a can't-lose guarantee.

Tax code letters and what they mean

L The most widespread coding where you receive the basic allowance - the amount everyone can earn before income tax starts.

P and V Normally used for pension payments, they indicate that you are aged 65-74 or 75 and over respectively. It tells the person paying you that you qualify for a higher tax allowance due to your age.

K You have used up all your tax allowances. This code might apply if you have a number of taxable perks, such as a company car and a private healthcare insurance policy.

BR and DO You get no allowances against your income because they have been used elsewhere. This can apply to someone with several employers. Always check that you are getting your allowance somewhere.

T Used where there is some uncertainty or the tax office needs to review your code. Question this.

SAYE is not automatic. Companies have to initiate a scheme – most big stock market-quoted concerns have a plan – and then, once it is established, offer you the chance to save between £5 and £250 each month into the contract. You agree to save for either three or five years (if you go for five years, you can leave your money for a further two to make seven).

When the SAYE plan starts, the company announces a starting share price – it can be anywhere between the stock market price on day one and 20 per cent below that.

Your money goes into a special bank or building society account where it grows at a set rate of interest, tax-free. On the expiry date, you compare the share price with the starting value.

- **If the share price has gone up,** you take the shares, which you can then sell or keep as you wish. Your salary is not taxed for this gain although you may be liable for capital gains tax (CGT) when you sell if your profit is large.
- **If the share price fell** over the contract period, you walk away from the shares deal, but you keep your savings plus the tax-free interest that you have earned instead.

This contract ends if you leave the company, although there are special rules if your departure is due to retirement, illness, redundancy or death.

Money saving tip

Anyone with big gains on a SAYE deal can sidestep capital gains tax by splitting the sale over two or more tax years to make the best use of the annual CGT exemption.

❝ The simplest and most widespread tax-saving scheme is Save As You Earn, which comes with a can't-lose guarantee. ❞

Working for yourself

An increasing number now work for themselves, often as a part-time addition to a full-time job elsewhere. Knowing what you can claim for and what is off-limits could slash your tax bill – and avoid problems.

THE TAX BILL

Your tax bill will be based on what you earn from customers less the costs you have incurred in running your business, so be sure to record the following expenditure items – keep receipts or other proof wherever possible. Items classed as expenditure can include:

- Contribution towards hardware, such as a computer or camera, even if you bought it before starting your business.
- Payments made to others.

 Selling on online auction sites (or at car boot sales, auctions or similar outlets) counts as self-employment if you buy items with the intention of selling them on at a profit. This does not apply if you are simply disposing of your embarrassing albums or your unwanted student books – items you bought for your own use and now no longer want or need.

- Your cost of premises – or a proportion of your heating, lighting, cleaning, insurance and general maintenance if you work from your home.
- Reasonable amounts for meals and overnight stays if you have to work away from your base.
- Fares on buses, trains, taxis, planes and boats when on business.
- Car expenses or a reasonable proportion of your costs if your car is also used privately or 20p a mile for a bicycle.
- Parking fees (but not parking tickets).
- Accountancy costs.
- Repairs and replacements.
- Advertising.
- Phone costs, mobile phone bills, broadband, postage, stationery.

Avoid a £100 penalty by registering your new business with Her Majesty's Revenue & Customs within three months of starting – call 0845 915 4515 for details.

❝ You can claim on hardware bought before you began in business. ❞

Putting your family on the payroll

You can reduce your own tax bill when self-employed (or owning a small company) by employing your spouse, civil partner or family members in the business. This way, others in your household may be able to use their personal tax allowances. This could make the difference between you paying as much as 41 per cent in taxes and national insurance and paying nothing.

But the work has to be genuine, within the capability of the person in your household (and not in contravention of rules that control work for young people) that you employ and paid for at a reasonable rate. Paying a 15-year-old child a few pounds an hour for basic clerical or manual tasks would be reasonable. Paying her or him £200 an hour for 'legal advice' or 'accountancy' would not wash.

Her Majesty's Revenue & Customs is targeting couples who try to reduce their tax bill by 'inventing' a job for a non-working spouse.

Case Study   Maureen

Maureen runs an agency from her home supplying domestic staff. She has two teenage children – James, 17, and Gina, 15. During their school holidays, Maureen offers James £5 an hour for two hours a week to sort out her filing mess she has accumulated and she gives Gina the same amount to carry out an audit of the cleaning materials she stores. She pays each one of them £500 over the year – a total of £1,000. These were jobs she used to do herself when the children were smaller. As a top-rate taxpayer, the £1,000 was previously taxed at 40 per cent (plus 1 per cent national insurance surcharge). In the hands of her children, it is tax-free as the amounts fall within their own tax-free allowances. The family has saved £410.

SHOULD I REGISTER FOR VAT?

Every year, the government publishes the level of sales (known to accountants as turnover) above which businesses have to register for Value Added Tax (VAT). This threshold is currently around £66,000. If you fail to register when you should,

For more information on tax and children, see pages 183–5 later in this chapter.

Taxing matters

167

there are fines depending on your turnover and how far behind you are in joining the scheme.

Once you are registered, you have to charge your customers 17.5 per cent extra on most items (5 per cent on some safety and environmental goods and 0 per cent on some food, books, magazines and newspapers and children's clothes), including your labour. This can make the goods and services you supply more expensive than the same items from someone who is not VAT registered.

Staying out of the VAT net

VAT registration is triggered by your sales figures, not your profits. In some cases you may be able to get your sales figures down while keeping your profits up by leaving it up to your customers to buy items instead of you doing it yourself.

Take the example of a central heating installer who earns £1,000 every week installing systems costing £6,000. If this person bought the systems at the local plumbing supplies shop and then billed the customer, the annual turnover would be substantially over the threshold. But if the customer went to the same store and ordered all the material and paid for it, then the installer would only have an annual turnover of labour charges – about £50,000. So no VAT would have to be charged.

The installer could either be £175 (the VAT on £1,000) more competitive than a VAT-registered rival or earn some more money by charging the same as the rival.

Flat-rate VAT scheme

If your customers are all VAT registered, they are quite happy to pay VAT as they can reclaim it. If you are in this situation and your turnover is under £150,000 you might be able to boost your income by signing up to the flat-rate VAT scheme. VAT traders can normally subtract the VAT on goods they buy in for their businesses (called the input) from the output VAT that they charge their customers.

But some businesses have very little taxable input – for example, a management consultant or a private detective or a specialist building worker. Nevertheless, they can save money by registering for VAT even when they don't have to.

By opting for the flat-rate scheme, companies such as this can no longer claim their input. Instead, they deduct a fixed part of their turnover and keep the rest tax-free. The fixed percentage varies according to the trade – it can, however, work out as a cash bonus of up to £1,000 a year compared with someone who is not registered.

 To find out more about the flat-rate, and other VAT methods of payment, go to www.hmrc.gov.uk and click on the link in the 'businesses and corporations' box.

Claim all the credits you can

There are a number of benefits credits – often means-tested – on offer from the government or your local authority. Most work on the basis that you have to ask for them or you won't get – there is often no automatic entitlement.

NATIONAL INSURANCE CREDITS

National insurance deductions from your earnings build up your contributions record for non-means-tested benefits, of which the state pension is the most important. If you have a significant gap in your record, such as missing several years altogether or missing several weeks each year for a long period, you may find your state retirement pension is cut or, in extreme cases, not paid at all.

Most people build up their national insurance record through deductions from their salary. But in certain circumstances you can apply for credits towards your record, even when you are not in work (or not earning enough each week for a national insurance deduction). These credits are free of charge, but can build up to a substantial proportion of your eventual pension.

❝Missing many payments could affect your state retirement pension.❞

Credits are added to your contribution record when you are:

- A full-time carer – this can include looking after your own children (see the 'Home responsibilities protection' box, overleaf).
- Out of work and signing on at the jobcentre, whether or not you are receiving jobseeker's allowance.
- Incapable of work through illness based on a medical certificate (but not if your employer continues to pay you).
- Aged 16–19 and in full-time education (less any weeks – perhaps a holiday job – where you earn enough to pay national insurance).
- Attending certain educational and training courses when you are over 19 – this does not include university and similar degree courses.
- Receiving statutory maternity pay or statutory adoption pay.
- On jury service (where your employer is not paying you for your time).
- Men that are aged 60–65 who are not in employment – generally those who took early retirement or are on state benefits.

Home responsibilities protection

This is a form of national insurance credit that helps parents and carers to satisfy the contribution conditions for long-term benefits, most importantly the state retirement pension. Instead of adding to your contribution record, it reduces the number of years that you would have had to pay national insurance to qualify for a state pension, which may add up to much the same in the end. You receive this protection if you are caring for someone with disabilities or for a child under 16 years.

Some national insurance credits will be given automatically – such as when you are on jobseeker's allowance. But if you stop work, for example, to take care of a disabled adult, or you are sick or on jury service, you will have to tell the national insurance office as it will not know in any other way. National insurance is part of Her Majesty's Revenue & Customs (HMRC), the overall tax and benefits organisation. Check any refusal to give you credits you believe should be yours with Citizens Advice or similar organisation (for contact information, see below).

The result is that when you reach the state pension age, you will get a higher weekly amount than if you have not bothered with national insurance credits. And that will continue for the rest of your life.

MARRIED WOMEN WHO PAY LESS, GET NOTHING

Women who were married (or widowed) before 12 May 1977 can opt to save money by selecting the married women's reduced rate national insurance contribution. But this is a case of pay less, get less. There is a whole raft of benefits that are excluded for those who decide to save with this lower-level payment of which the most important is the state retirement pension in their own right – they will have to depend on their husband's contributions.

Women in this category can opt to go onto the full payment. But before doing so, they should ask the local tax office for an illustration of what they will gain and what they will lose. For someone just a year or two away from retirement, it may make more sense to save the money rather than increase national insurance payments, although for most younger women (and some could still be in their late forties), it may make sense to switch.

❝ Tell the national insurance office if you stop work to care for a disabled person. ❞

 To find out more about national insurance and other tax credits, go to the HMRC website: www.hmrc.gov.uk and follow the links or go directly to http://taxcredits.direct.gov.uk/ or call the tax credit helpline on 0845 300 3900. To find your local Citizens Advice office, go to www.citizensadvice.org.uk.

CHILD TAX CREDIT

This is paid to households that have at least one child and where the total household income (taking in both parents in a two-parent family) is less than £58,000 a year. This goes up to £66,000 where a child is below the age of one, and it can be higher in certain circumstances where parents incur substantial childcare costs. It is worth at least £545 – double that, or £1,090, where a child is under one. For most families, it is paid at this standard rate irrespective of the number of children.

You can continue to claim child tax credit until the child reaches 16 – or up to 19 if he or she is still in full-time education at school, sixth-form college or similar institution, but not in higher education such as a university.

You could get more if you are on a lower income and there are additional special payments if you have a child with a disability.

WORKING TAX CREDIT

This is a means-tested benefit that can boost the income of those on moderate to low pay whether they are single or living with a partner and irrespective of whether or not they have children. It could be worth £1,665 per year – or more if someone in your household has certain special needs.

Again, you have to apply (see the box at the foot of page 170) – it won't be given automatically. Working tax credit can be complicated, so ask your local Citizens Advice Bureau or similar organisation for help.

> **" Working tax credit could be worth £1,665 per year, or more if someone in the household has some special needs. "**

Claiming child tax credit

Although the child tax credit applies to the great majority of families, you have to apply for this as the tax office, who administers the benefit, has no records either of total household income or of which households have children. If you miss out making an application at the right time, you can still apply, although a successful claim can only be backdated by three months.

Failing to apply means failing to get this money - hardly a great way to save! There is no penalty if you claim and are turned down.

Once you are on the system for child tax credit, you should receive a renewal pack once a year where you have to say if your household income has fallen or risen (and by how much!) since the last time you filled it in.

PENSION CREDIT

Pension credit is a means-tested state benefit that you have to apply for – there is no automatic entitlement to receive it. Its purpose is to give everyone aged sixty or over a minimum weekly income irrespective of earnings or pensions. This goes up each year, but it is around £125 for a single person and about £190 for those living with a partner (higher for those with disabilities).

There are special additional allowances for those who have built savings or second pensions to help fund their retirement – certain sums from these sources are taken out of the equation.

HOUSING BENEFIT

This is administered by your local council. It gives help with your rent and your council tax bill if you are on a low income and have less than £16,000 in savings. Your local council will give you more details.

Help with council tax

You get a 25 per cent discount if there is only one taxable adult in the household. Students on full-time courses are exempt. So a house full of students (and exclusively students) would pay no council tax. You have to apply to your local council for any reduction from the standard council tax rate.

Claiming pension credit

Your actual income, including any work and pensions but not housing benefit, is calculated and it is assumed that your savings generate 10 per cent a year (even if they don't). The value of your home, if you own it, is not taken into the calculation. The state then makes up the gap between that amount and the pension credit level in force that year.

If you qualify, applications can be backdated for up to 12 months. Furthermore, you can fill in the forms up to four months before you might start to be eligible.

It may be worth applying even if you think you might only get a very small sum as pension credit is a 'passport' to other benefits including housing benefit and council tax benefit (see left), which could be worth more to money savers than the extra they might get from the pension credit.

❝ A quarter of the council tax bill is cut for households with only one taxable adult. ❞

Should we get married?

Tying the knot is an emotional issue outside the scope of a money saving book as it's all down to individual preferences (and that includes contracting a civil partnership as all the rules that apply to heterosexual marriages also apply to single-sex partnerships). But should you decide to, there are tax advantages.

Tax relief for married couples has disappeared except for some people now in their seventies or older. Since the early 1990s, married couples have been treated as separate people for tax purposes. And means-tested benefits make no distinction between those who are married and those who live together as spouses (known as co-habiting). However, there are some financial advantages and a few drawbacks in getting hitched legally.

TELL THE WORLD YOU'RE ENGAGED

Whether you do it in the traditional way via a posh person's newspaper and or tell all your friends on Facebook, becoming engaged means that you can tell your older and richer relations and friends that they can save up to 40 per cent of the cost of the wedding gifts they plan to give you provided they hand them over no later than the day you marry.

Alternatively, and admittedly this is not very romantic, you can inform them they can give you a more valuable present than they otherwise would have done because of tax benefits (you may have to phrase it carefully for the full money saving potential). If your parents are well enough off, you could suggest that they could give you £5,000 for the cost of £3,000. The reason for this is that certain gifts given to celebrate a wedding/civil partnership are exempt from **inheritance tax**.

Your parents can each give the about-to-be-wed couple £5,000 – it does not matter if you are illegitimate, legitimate, adopted or a step-child. Grandparents can fork out £2,500 each, while unrelated people can give a generous £1,000 – and it all goes out of the giver's inheritance tax bill, which could be 40 per cent if they kept the money and then died.

Jargon buster

Inheritance tax A tax payable on amounts you might inherit on the donor's death, or were otherwise given in the seven years preceding their death

Tax-free allowance The amount we can all earn before paying income tax

SAVING ON SAVINGS TAX

To do this, you have to trust your other half and be prepared to divulge your finances to your partner. Although there is nothing you can currently do if one partner does not use their **tax-free allowance**, where one partner is paying tax at a higher rate than the other, you can save tax money by transferring assets from the higher taxed to the lower (or zero) taxed. This could be from the top rate to the basic rate or the top rate to no tax or the basic rate to no tax.

When it comes to paying the tax on interest on your savings, then, provided the transfer from one to the other is definite, the rate will be that of the new owner, which should then be less than the original owner. Overall, the household saves money on its total tax bill.

The downside is that once you have done this, the giver has no more control over the money. But you can sidestep this with a compromise. Set up the account in joint names so each can draw upon it. HMRC will treat half the interest going to the higher tax-rated partner and half going to the lower.

TAKING CAPITAL FROM YOUR GAINS

Legally hitched partners can transfer assets between themselves at any time without any tax worries or concerns.

This can be during their lifetime or on the death of one partner.

If you have assets such as shares that can be transferred easily (or divided) between two partners, then it can save up to around £4,000 a year on **capital gains tax**. The way it works is that each partner has their own individual annual capital gains tax exemption – it's currently nearly £10,000. If a taxable gain falls within the exemption, it's tax-free. Otherwise, it will most probably be taxed at 18 per cent from 6 April 2008.

Those people who have enough gains on selling shares or other assets can double the tax-free amount by using both their tax-free slices provided they transfer the assets from one to another before the sale.

Jargon buster

Capital gains tax A tax paid on profits you make when you sell assets, including shares, second homes and works of art. The tax changes radically on 6 April 2008 when a complex system is replaced by a flat 18 per cent tax on gains above your annual exemption level (this changes each year but is roughly just under £10,000 per person)

 For more information on tax savings see the *Which? Essential Guides Tax Handbook 2008/9* (published 5 May 2008, or see the 2007/8 edition) and *Giving and Inheriting*.

Case Study Jenny and Emma

Jenny and Emma contracted a civil partnership. Jenny has shares that she intends selling in early spring so the couple can move into a larger home for the summer. She calculates that her capital tax gain will be about £40,000. Jenny transfers half her holding to Emma. As they are married, there is no tax to worry about on this move.

They then sell half their holdings just before the end of the tax year on 5 April.

Each has a £10,000 taxable gain - more or less equal to their annual exemption. Then on 6 April, they sell the other half of their holdings. As this is a new tax year, they start off again with another tax-free slice (and probably at a slightly higher amount as the level tends to go up each year). The saving amounts over the two tax years to around £8,000 - enough to pay for some smart furniture for the new home!

ARE THERE BENEFITS FROM BEING UNWED?

One potential saving is that if each partner owns their own house, staying unwed means that each can keep (and later sell) the property as their own principal residence. This means that each sale would be free of capital gains tax. Alternatively, one of a couple living together unmarried – the one without any property ownership – could move on to buying a second home, knowing that a subsequent sale would be free of capital gains tax.

As a married couple, they could only have one home that would be tax-free on a sale (although you do normally get three years after the marriage in which to sell one of the properties capital gains tax-free). This could be useful where the couple want to keep two homes – perhaps one in a city and one in the country. This could eventually save up to 40 per cent of the profit made on the property.

Tapping into your family wealth

Even if you have no intention of marriage , you can always remind better-off family members and friends that they can give up to £3,000 a year without any inheritance tax worries and go back 12 months if they omitted to do this a year ago. To get £3,000 from the will of someone who has to pay inheritance tax would mean them leaving you £5,000. They can also give countless gifts of up to £250 each year to other people.

> **❝ If each partner owns their own house, staying unwed means each can keep and later sell the property as their principal residence. ❞**

Cutting your tax bill

You will not be delivered tax savings on a plate. But paying less tax legitimately is not difficult provided you are prepared to plan ahead and fill in a few forms. Your employer can also help with perks, ranging from a tax-free annual party to paying around half the cost of a new bicycle.

WHAT YOUR EMPLOYER CAN DO FOR YOU

Most of what you earn from your work, including overtime, bonuses, commission, tips and holiday pay, counts towards your taxable income. But there are some payments and non-cash benefits that your employer can give you that escape the tax net.

As an employee, you can save tax in a number of ways. But none are automatic. Your employer has to agree to provide you with them. In some cases, your employer may be unaware of the full range of possibilities – you may have to adopt the same tactics as the staff at a number of organisations by going out and actively persuading their firms to set up some or all of the following tax-free perks. Don't forget that benefits such as childcare can affect tax credits.

Organisations employing five or more people must offer a stakeholder pension plan, but they don't have to pay into it for you.

Saving tax through pension payments

If you work for a firm or organisation that employs five or more people, the employer has to offer you a stakeholder pension plan. That does not mean much – the boss is not obliged to put anything in it for you. But many employers go one step further than this legal minimum and pay regular pension contributions to employees who want to join their scheme.

Joining a pension plan is not obligatory. Most employers will want you to make a contribution from your salary – often 5 or 6 per cent of your salary – as a condition of membership. Few will increase your salary if you turn down the pension membership. But it is equivalent to a salary increase – admittedly one you won't be able to enjoy until you reach at least 55 (it's 50 until 2010). This increase is often worth more as you get older and nearer to retirement.

It is only worth turning down a pension plan if you are among the low paid (an income of less than £12,000 per year) and expect to remain on that level until you retire – having a pension might affect means-tested state benefits (assuming the present system does not change, which is a big assumption if you're forty years away from retirement – and not a sure bet even if you are in your forties or early fifties).

But otherwise, go for the pension – it is as near to free money as you can get. Your employer's money is a boost to your income while the money you put in escapes income tax. For a top-rate taxpayer (someone earning around £43,000 or more), every £1 you give up from your spendable income becomes worth £1.67 in a pension plan. For basic rate taxpayers, it's £1.28 for each £1 (it will be £1.25 from 2009). And once your money is in a pension plan, it grows in a largely tax-free environment, resulting in a further saving over most other investment options.

Anything you add to your workplace pension from your own resources or pay into another pension plan is also boosted by the tax relief. In general terms, you can now pay your entire annual earnings from work into a pension – there are special rules for those who are very highly paid.

The pension plan is effectively a long-term boost to your savings that will pay a regular income each month when you retire plus – if you want – a tax-free lump sum.

Money saving tip

If you can afford it, you can help a non-working spouse, partner, child, grandchild or, in fact, anyone under 75 towards a pension via a stakeholder plan. You can put up to £3,600 a year into one for someone else, but it will not cost you that much because the basic-rate tax comes off leaving you to find up to £2,808 (£2,880 from 2009).

❝ Joining a pension plan is as near to free money as you can get, and every £1 you pay in is worth £1.67 because it is tax-free. **❞**

Subsidised staff canteen

Your employer can provide low-cost or even free food for you at work provided that a few rules are followed. You are not taxed on this perk. The employer would normally operate a staff canteen – it could even be two canteens as the rules allow one for blue collar staff and one for while collar employees as long as the food is the same in both and one or the other of the canteens is open to all staff. Your employer could also arrange a private dining-room facility at a local restaurant.

For more information about pensions, see the *Which? Essential Guide Pension Handbook.*

Employees can also receive up to 15p per working day (a sum unchanged since the 1960s) in luncheon vouchers tax-free. If your boss gives you more than 15p, the first 15p is still tax-free.

Staff party

Companies can treat employees to a staff party provided the total per head expenditure does not top £150. This can be at Christmas, in the summer or at any other time. There is nothing to stop more than one party a year – provided that the total spend does not exceed £150 per head.

Childcare facilities

Employers can provide workplace nurseries or crèches as a tax-free perk provided it is exclusively for employees. It can, however, be shared with employees of other companies and it does not have to be on company premises. An alternative, where the boss wants to help employees with small children but does not want or cannot set up a nursery or a nursery share with other firms, is to give up to £55 a week in tax-free vouchers, which can be spent at an approved childcare facility.

❝ If you pay a lot in phone bills it may be worth accepting a slightly lower salary in return for personal use of a company phone. ❞

Sports and recreational facilities

Providing everything from a running track to a club where you can play pool via a staff orchestra is a totally tax-free perk provided the facilities are not shared with non-employees. So you can't have tax-free membership of your local gym or sports club.

Mobile phones

Employees can use mobile phones supplied by their firms free of tax for personal as well as work-related use. If your phone bills are large, it may be worth your while accepting a slightly lower salary and having a phone instead. Some firms offer a free mobile phone as a choice on a flexible (often called 'flexi') benefits menu – where you can opt for a number of selections such as medical care or longer holidays or extra salary.

Long-service awards

You can have a tax-free lump sum once you have spent at least 20 years with one employer at a maximum rate of £50 per year of service – so 20 years could give £1,000 extra outside of income tax.

Company suggestion schemes

If you come up with an idea that has a genuine commercial value to your employer, and it is not in your job descriptions to think up ideas, your employer can reward you with up to £5,000, free of tax.

Working at home

Those people who regularly work at home with the agreement of their employer can claim up to £2 a week tax-free. This can be more if you provide proof of additional costs.

Medical check-ups

These are tax-free when they are related to health and safety at work. If your work requires regular VDU use or any other work where your eyesight might be at risk, your employer has to offer you a free eye test once every two years and the cost of a basic pair of suitable glasses if the optician says you need them (or cash help towards a more expensive pair).

Expenses to cover relocation

If you have to move home for your job, you can reclaim up to £8,000 relocation expenses free of tax from your employer to cover your costs.

Foreign visits

If you have to work overseas for periods of at least sixty days at a time, your employer can give you airoplane tickets so that your spouse or civil partner plus any children under 18 yeears of age can visit you. This perk is limited to twice a year.

Help with transport

The costs of your daily travel to work normally comes out of your taxed income, but your employer can help in some cases by reimbursing in full:

- **Disabled person's travelling expenses.** These can be paid tax-free to employees with a registered disability.
- **Late-night taxi travel.** This can be a tax-free perk when it is deemed necessary for the employee's health and safety. But it cannot be offered to someone whose regular working pattern includes unsociable hours; it has to be occasional, for instance when you are forced to stay unusually late.
- **Mileage allowance payments.** You can have up to 40p a mile tax-free if you use your own car for work purposes (but not for commuting to and from the workplace) up to 10,000 miles. The rate drops to 25p a mile after that. Motorbikes get 24p a mile. If you are paid less than this, you can claim the balance against your personal tax. Someone driving 1,000 miles and only receiving 10p a mile could claim 1,000 x 30p = £300 from their taxable income. This might be a better deal than a company car as many employers will now boost your salary instead of giving you this perk. The choice can be complex depending on

If you are looking for tax advice and can't afford to pay a professional adviser, you might be eligible for help from TaxAid (www.taxaid.org.uk). For more information, see also page 211.

Taxing matters

Getting a bike for around half price

Under the Green Transport Plan, you can buy a bike (conventional or electric-motor aided) for around half price, provided your employer signs up to a 'cycle to work' scheme with a bike retailer (most shops belong to a national scheme although some big bike shop chains operate their own plan).

Buying your bike

- You choose your bike plus accessories that can be justified on safety grounds, such as lights, helmet, high-visibility clothing and locks, and the shop sends the bill to your employer (some schemes offer you a voucher for a set amount which you give to the shop).

- There is no limit on the value of the bike although many employers set a £1,000 ceiling. But don't expect any discount on the list price for membership of a local cycling club or scheme – the shop has to give the scheme operator 10 per cent.

- Your employer then divides the total cost of the bike package (usually by 12) and charges you one payment each month for a year.

- The clever bit is that this money comes from the very top of your salary slip before any tax or national insurance is deducted, so you are buying your new bike with untaxed money. Besides giving you a tax-free loan, your boss also absorbs the VAT if the employer is VAT-registered.

- During the year, the bike legally belongs to your employer, who leases it to you. If you leave, you lose any benefit.

- At the end of the year, you pay the employer a small fee to buy the bike outright. Depending on your personal tax rate and whether the employer can reclaim VAT (most can), you end up paying around 50–60 per cent of the bike's original value.

❝ Money for a bike is deducted from your salary before tax or national insurance, so it is a tax-free loan, and your employer can pay the VAT. ❞

> **"** Her Majesty's Revenue & Customs offers a number of tax-free perks to encourage cycling, including breakfasts and shower and changing facilities. **"**

Using your bike

- You are supposed to use the bike for regular commuting to work. But cycling to the local station and then taking the train is acceptable for longer distances.

- You cannot claim the 20p a mile usage if you buy the bike this way.

This whole process is known as salary sacrifice. The purchase reduces your annual income, so your pension benefits could be cut and your earnings for mortgage purposes will be lower. You could, of course, always put the equivalent of your bike savings into a pension plan – free of tax.

Further cyclist tax-free perks

Her Majesty's Revenue & Customs offers a number of tax-free perks to encourage cycling. These include:

- Free showers and changing facilities at work.

- The oddity of the 'cyclist's breakfast' where those who arrive on two wheels can have a free meal (there is no cost limit so it could be champagne and caviar) on six occasions a year.

- Where you use your own bike for work-related travel, you can claim up to 20p a mile tax-free (this is the equivalent of the 40p paid to car drivers).

the value of the car, its carbon emissions, and how far you drive for the employer and how much you use the vehicle privately. But a company benefits specialist will be able to help you on making your decision.

- **Interest-free loans of up to £5,000.** You pay no tax on the value of the interest you would otherwise have to pay. These loans are normally given for season-ticket purchase. If the loan is more than £5,000, you have to pay tax on the entire perk, not just the amount over £5,000.

> **❝ Loans can be made for the purchase of season tickets, but if the amount goes over £5,000, you pay tax on the entire perk, not the excess. ❞**

- **Workplace parking.** This could be a shared car park or a public car park for which your employer picks up the bill.
- **Green commuting.** This includes the provision of certain bus services and perks for cyclists (see pages 180–1).

 There are a number of website calculators, such as www.comcar.co.uk or www.theaa.com, that can help you work out if a company car is worth having or not.

Tax and children

Children can become taxpayers before they can learn to walk. But they also have a personal tax allowance - the amount that can be earned tax-free - from the moment they are born. This can save them up to around £1,000 a year in income tax, but they - or you on their behalf - have to ask for it.

WHOSE MONEY IS IT?

Money given to children belongs to the children themselves. But from Her Majesty's Revenue & Customs' (HMRC) point of view, there is a big difference between money that comes from parents and money that comes from anyone else, such as grandparents, adult brothers and sisters, aunts, uncles, godparents and family friends.

HMRC is concerned that parents may give their children money to ensure it is taxed at a lower rate than it would otherwise be if it was still owned by adults. The first £5,400 (the personal allowance level whose precise level changes each year) or so of interest on savings for a child who has no other income is tax-free.

So money that is given by parents remains taxable as though it still belongs to the parent until the child reaches 18 years. HMRC does not want to hit small sums. Therefore, where the interest income from a parent's gift is no more than £100, it is tax-free. Each parent can give a sum that generates this £100. The catch is that if the interest rose to £101 – say interest rates rise or the child reinvests the interest – there is tax to be paid on the entire amount at the parent's top tax rate, not just that above £100.

> **❝ HMRC views money from parents as different to cash from anyone else, including family members. ❞**

 To get professional advice from an independent financial adviser in your area, go to www.unbiased.co.uk.

Invest in tax-free areas

Parents could save tax money on gifts to children by investing their money in areas that are tax free, have minimal tax or which enable any tax payable to be put off into the future when the child becomes an adult and the tax burden moves off the parent's shoulders. These can include:

- **National Savings certificates** – they are tax-free.
- **National Savings Children's Bonus Bonds** – these are tax-free.
- **Insurance bonds** – any tax can be deferred until the day the bond is encashed.
- **Friendly Society savings plans** (limited to £25 a month) – tax-free while in the fund with the proceeds paid out without any tax liability.

66 Money for investment purposes can be separated from the child's other money with a simple form of trust. 99

While these investments have tax advantages, they may not be suitable for the individual. Always take independent financial advice if you are in doubt.

- Share portfolios focused on growth shares – any **dividends** are paid free of basic-rate tax. Growth shares typically have low dividends although they can be risky.

A child's investments

Money from any other source can be invested by the child in whatever is considered suitable. Grandparents and others who give money for investment can ensure it is separated from their own money and designated for the child with a simple form of **trust** – the most basic is called a 'bare trust'. Banks, building societies and many stock market-based investment companies will produce a form that you can use for this purpose.

TELLING HMCR YOU'RE A NON-TAXPAYER

Whether you are a non-earning adult or a child, you will need to tell HMRC of your non-taxpayer status to ensure your interest on a bank or building society account is paid to you without any deduction for tax – with few exceptions, accounts take off 20 per cent for basic-rate income tax before they pay out the annual or monthly interest due.

Form R85

You do this by filling in form R85 when you open an account or shortly afterwards. This should ensure your interest is paid without a deduction. Parents can fill in the form for children who are too young to understand the form. You need one R85 for each account you have, although once in place,

Jargon buster

Dividend Regular payment from shares

Trust A legal arrangement where one or more people (the trustees) hold money or assets (the trust property) to be used for the benefit of one or more other people (the beneficiaries). The trustees can set conditions on how the trust property is held and used

it lasts from year to year until or unless you rescind it.

While suitable for children and adults, the R85 suddenly stops – usually without warning – when a child reaches 16, even if the child is continuing in education and is not going to work. The only way around this is to renew each R85 on the child's 16th birthday. It then continues past 18 until the account holder earns enough money from all sources to become a taxpayer.

Form R40

If you miss out by not filling in the R85, ask for form R40 – it's a way of telling HMRC that you want to get back the interest you should not have paid in the first place. You have up to six years to do this. The refund will have interest added

to it – at whatever HMRC's interest rate is at the time.

CHILD TRUST FUNDS

All children born since September 2002 receive £250 on birth (£500 for those born into lower income families) towards a tax-free fund. There will be a further £250 or £500 when she or he reaches seven. The money cannot be touched, in normal circumstances, until the child reaches 18 years. To make best use of it, parents have to activate the money by investing it in an approved cash or stock market fund.

The money saving opportunity arises because parents – and anyone else – can invest up to £100 a month (£1,200 a year) without incurring any taxation. This is in addition to amounts parents may put away for their offspring in other tax-free products.

> **❝ Children born since September 2002 receive at least £250, with a further sum on their seventh birthday. ❞**

 You can get forms R40 and R85 from your local tax office (see phone book) or from the HMRC website: www.hmrc.gov.uk.

Paying your tax on time

This section will not help you save money on your tax bill, but it will prevent you paying penalties and interest, which could add hundreds or more to your annual tax outgoings.

Two-thirds of taxpayers need never go near an income tax form, although they may need to apply for child tax credit. These 20 million or so, whether they are in work or receiving a pension large enough to be taxed will have all their tax affairs dealt with through PAYE – Pay As You Earn.

The other one in three has to complete an annual tax form known as self-assessment. Once you are on the self-assessment system, you should receive a form every year – usually in April for the tax year that has just ended.

FILLING IN A SELF-ASSESSMENT FORM

But if you don't receive a form, that's no excuse not to fill one in. Her Majesty's Revenue & Customas (HMRC) expects you to know that you have to complete the form, irrespective of whether it has contacted you. Failure to do this could lead to penalties and interest.

The main groups who have to fill in a self-assessment form

- Higher-rate taxpayers with any savings or investment income.
- Anyone with a taxable perk, such as a company car or private medical insurance plan.
- Those with earnings from self-employment.
- Partners in businesses.
- Company directors.
- Those with foreign or other untaxed income.

There are others as well – effectively anyone whose tax affairs are not the plainest of vanilla. The general rule is if you are in doubt, get a form and fill it out. There are no penalties for taking up more of HMRC's time than you strictly have to.

 To obtain your self-assessment forms, go to www.hmrc.gov.uk and follow the links in the 'Individuals and employees' box to 'self-assessment'.

The forms are all available online (see bottom of page 186) – and it is usually to your advantage to file online.

You have some choices before hitting the penalty zone for being late.

Filing a paper form

- You can file your paper form by 30 September and get HMRC to calculate how much you owe (or how much rebate is due to you). This will save you the £100–£150 you would have to pay an accountant to deal with even a very simple form.
- You can work it out yourself either using specialist software or HMRC's own (not very easy to follow) paper-based calculation guide – and file by 31 October.

In both cases, you will not have to pay anything you owe until 31 January.

Filing online

The easiest way is to file online either using HMRC's software or buying a specialist package, which is approved by HMRC (costing around £25). This way, you get to know immediately how much you owe/are due for a rebate. You have until 31 January to do this and to pay if you owe anything. Online customers also get rebates more quickly.

Meeting the deadlines

Failure to comply – even by one day – means an instant £100 fine (the amount is being looked at as it has not changed for over ten years so it may go up soon). There's a further £100 six months later

on if you still have not filed and paid up. And all the time interest is mounting, with a 5 per cent interest surcharge as well after one month, with a further 5 per cent from 1 August.

If the deadline is upon you and you are in a mess with your paperwork, then try to work it out very roughly and overpay. You cannot be penalised if you owe nothing. You can later reclaim your overpayment and any penalties you might have had to pay.

TAX REBATE COMPANIES

People employed in the UK for a short time only, often foreign students or backpackers who work for a month or two, may not earn enough to pay tax. In many cases, they will have no tax records when they start so the employer will deduct basic-rate tax as they are obliged to do by law. Some temporary workers could overpay by more than £1,000.

They will be the target of several tax rebate and tax refund companies. They often advertise in magazines and on websites read by short-term foreign workers, promising a 'no win, no fee' service that will get them all they are due from HMRC.

These firms also sometimes market themselves at retired people, offering to sort out any rebate, again on a no win, no fee basis.

However, they do carry out what they promise, although they do deduct anything between 25 and 40 per cent of the money they recover as their fee. That could be over £400.

You – or anyone you know who might be in this situation – can do exactly what they do for nothing. Obtain form R40 from the HMRC website (www.hmrc.gov.uk) and tell them that you have left the UK permanently for tax purposes when you fill it in. You can do this on form P85 – 'Leaving the United Kingdom'.

Sign this form to say you have left the country for good. Agreeing does not mean you can never return – you could always do some work in a year's time in a new tax period and get another rebate, as well as visiting the UK as a non-earner at any time.

> " HMRC have heard all the excuses before, including pets eating paperwork and earnings being dog track winnings. "

WHAT NOT TO DO!

HMRC have heard all the excuses and dodges before. They are well practised at knowing the difference between evasion and making an innocent technical mistake, such as mixing up two different forms of investment or failing to sign a form at the right place.

So trying to dodge taxes will cause you penalties and fines as well as interest. In some cases, you could end up in prison.

Here's a tiny selection of the stories they've heard all too often before:

- I didn't know I had to declare overseas earnings.
- I thought my offshore savings account was tax-free.
- I didn't know that I had earned that.
- My dog/rabbit/rat ate my paperwork so I can't fill in a form.
- I was paid in cash – that does not count.
- I didn't think tips were taxable.
- I didn't earn that money – I won it at the dog track.

Avoiding the scams

The flipside of saving money is losing it. Read on to discover more on sharp practices, barely legal scams, totally illegal swindles and those 'how can anyone be so stupid to fall for that?' tricks.

Sharp practices

All these are legal but will involve you in pointless expense. Some of the practices are 'chiselling' where companies reckon that while you won't miss a few pennies here and the odd pound or two there, they can make millions by getting many people to fall for these less than desirable trading methods.

THE RESTAURANT SERVICE CHARGE SCAM

Tipping is controversial. You are expected to add up to 20 per cent to the food and drinks bill in the United States but staff in some northern European countries think tipping is demeaning. And some customers hate paying these charges while others think it can be a good idea to encourage good service. Whatever your attitude, don't pay twice. Many restaurants add a service charge automatically (deduct it if you think the service was appalling) and then guide you to the voluntary additional service charge on the credit card machine. Don't fall for this. If you wish to leave a tip because service has not been added, waiting staff generally prefer cash to a credit card payment – it goes straight to them and does not attract VAT (although waiting staff have to pay income tax on tips).

CREDIT CARD SURCHARGES

Some companies charge you extra if you use a credit card. It's legal as long as they tell you in advance. This can be as much as 5 per cent – and whatever the level, it can often be higher on American Express than on Visa or Mastercard. But unless you really need the credit that month, or are feeling you really need the protection you get from credit card purchases if the company goes bust, it's rarely worth paying.

Holiday companies typically add 3–4 per cent for using a credit card yet, provided you deal with a UK tour operator or travel agent, you are protected by travel industry schemes so the additional Consumer Credit Act protection (which helps if the company you are dealing with goes bust) is unnecessary. Use a debit card instead.

 For more on the subject of good credit card usage, see pages 60-8.

BOOKING FEES

Theatres, cinemas, opera houses and museums often add a surcharge for booking tickets online or by phone even when it is actually cheaper for them to sell electronically than at the box office at the venue. A small fee such as £1 or £1.50 can be excused if tickets have to be posted to your home, but a per ticket surcharge where the more tickets you order at one time, the more you pay is just plain greedy and inexcusable. So try to use the box office wherever possible – there legally has to be somewhere where you can buy tickets at their face value.

DIRECTORY ENQUIRIES

The 118 numbers for finding out phone numbers are expensive, with some charging up to 60p for a connection and then up to 60p per minute thereafter, although usually a higher connection charge brings a lower per-minute fee. And costs from mobiles can be even higher. To add salt to your financial wound, you are charged even if the number cannot be found or the operator takes a long time or you end up being told the number is ex-directory.

You can often find numbers of many companies via Google or a similar search engine. And it's worth trying online sites

where you can search for free such as www.ukphonebook.com/. Going online can often help you avoid rip-off 0871, 0870 and 0845 numbers as well (see pages 112–13).

RINGTONES AND WALLPAPER

There's a whole industry out there seemingly dedicated to getting you to sign up for a constant supply of ringtones or mobile phone wallpaper. Phones come with a variety of tones for free, while you can make your own wallpaper using the camera. There is nothing wrong with the occasional purchase, but always check the small print first or you could be shelling out a fiver a week via your bill or from your phone credit on a contract you didn't know you had and wished you had never heard about.

COIN-COUNTING MACHINES

Supermarkets often provide machines where you can pour in coins and the machine tells you how much they are worth. But the typical machine charges 7.9 per cent and then may only give you vouchers to the value of the coins to spend in the store. The alternative is to ask your bank for coin bags (which are free) and then count your money out

 To find out the directory enquiry costs, go to the website www.118tracker.com, which has an up-to-date listing.

into the right amounts for these. Local shops are often glad to receive small change – it saves them having to pay their bank for it.

FEE-CHARGING CASH MACHINES

Unbelievably, people would rather spend £1.50 or £2 to withdraw as little as £10 from fee-charging cash machines when there are others that are free within a minute's walk. Avoiding them should be a matter of some simple pre-planning. Having them, especially at pubs and clubs, is just a way of getting you to bust your budget and spend more than you intended. Some machines in isolated locations do allow you to make one cost-free withdrawal a day of up to £10 or £20.

66 Unbelievably, some people will spend £2 to withdraw £10 rather than taking a short walk to a charge-free cash machine. 99

SAVINGS ACCOUNTS WITHDRAWAL FEES

Watch out for savings accounts that, if you make even a £1 withdrawal, offer 0 per cent interest on your whole nest egg for a complete month. These may offer good rates and instant withdrawals, but for every month you go without interest, you are effectively losing almost 0.5 per cent a year.

INSURANCE-SWITCHING FEES

Mortgage companies can legally insist you have buildings cover on properties where there is a loan. But much as they would wish to, they cannot insist you buy cover from them as you can often find a cheaper or more comprehensive policy elsewhere. Some say they will charge you a fee for letting you go elsewhere – usually £25. You cannot escape this but you can ask your new insurer to pay this for you – most will.

THE LOW/HIGH SUPERMARKET TECHNIQUE

Supermarkets may make a big play of really low prices on items you rarely if ever buy, hoping you think the store is good value. But once you are enticed in, you find all the items you want on a regular basis are really expensive.

 For more advice on other supermarket scams and how to make the most of your shopping forays, see pages 148–52.

Barely legal scams

Perpetrators of these scams would argue they are legal and that people who complain did not read the terms and conditions, but if you did, then you would probably never fall for them.

LOATHSOME LOTTERIES

Lotteries are popular. Millions buy National Lottery tickets and scratchcards every week, they purchase Premium Bonds (where you swap the chance of winning for the interest on your money), as well as buying tickets for charity draws. But although every entrant hopes for a good prize, they know the odds against the jackpot are astronomical – around 14 million to one for the National Lottery's main weekly draw.

They also know they can watch the main draw live on the television, so all the tickets, whatever their number combination, have an equal chance of winning. But some lotteries that you might hear about through the post or from a flyer falling out of a magazine offer huge prizes, such as £20,000 or a luxury car, and you are told that you are 'a guaranteed winner' and you have no need to buy a ticket. While these statements are true, they are nevertheless potentially misleading.

Unlike the mainstream National Lottery where you choose your number, these offer you a 'winning number'. You then have two choices. You can send a stamped addressed envelope to the promoter and be told what you have won. Alternatively, you can spend £9 on a six-minute-long £1.50-a-minute premium rate call to be told what your number has won.

In almost all cases, you will be told you have 'won' an almost worthless piece of jewellery or a low-specification digital camera (for which you'll have to fork out a further £10 for postage and packing). So you'll be spending £19 on a camera you will find is far less well appointed than the one on your mobile phone – or about £10 if you resist the temptation to call the phone line.

Some companies selling tacky goods such as the 'perpetual pentagram of protection' try to draw you into buying by offering a lottery on the side. Again, and these have been the subject of Office of Fair Trading official warnings, you are likely to end up with 'jewellery' that is probably cheaper than Christmas cracker contents.

❝ You might be a 'guaranteed winner', but your prize will be worth far less than the phone call required to claim it. ❞

POINTLESS POTIONS

Dieting involves determination and devotion to the gym or other method of exercising. Without pain, there will only be weight gain. But to read some of the claims of those people pushing potions, you could lose 10lb in the first week alone without any effort on your part.

One comes from 'Professor' Martin Huntingdon-Smith of Nuturhealth Care Trust in Belgium. Neither the professor nor the trust have ever been tracked down but enough people want an effort-free weight-loss programme (even though none exists) to make a fortune for those behind his '100% natural' pills, which cost £44.95 if you want to lose 17–22lb.

Then there is Slimtox whose publicty material features (although they were not aware of it) Elton John, the Duchess of York, Michael Jackson and Robbie Williams as apparent endorsers of this magic potion. This comes from the same stable as miracle slimming products Lipo-Slim and Cellu-Svelte.

Slimtox, which makes unsubstantiated medical and scientific claims, breaks just about every rule in the Advertising Standards Authority (ASA) code. Slimming products should make clear the need for diet and exercise – Slimtox says you can eat five meals a day and need not exercise or diet.

ASA rules ban claims of precise weight loss in a set period – Slimtox 'guarantees' 33kg (over 5 stone) in two months. Claims should be compatible with good medical practice – no more than 1kg (2lb) loss a week.

These are all posted in the UK. The Royal Mail says it cannot check what is in envelopes.

To succeed, the two schemes listed above rely on many people sending in relatively small amounts of money. If you fall for them, it's not great but you may be able to chalk it up to 'experience'. But you can lose very serious money in barely legal schemes.

PRACTICALLY WORTHLESS PROPERTY

Here you are contacted by a company that tells you a number of obvious facts, such as there is a housing shortage and this will need more homes to be built. These are backed up by statistics and articles taken from newspapers.

In addition, everyone knows that land that has planning permission for residential building is worth many times more than land that is zoned only for farming requirements.

Adding these together, some companies are contacting people claiming that they have the expertise to know which land, currently without planning

> ❝ 'Land banking' could work in theory, but the get-out is the small print warning that planning permission is not guaranteed. ❞

permission, is likely to get it within 'the next two to three years or even sooner'. And once it has permission, then its value will soar, so you will multiply your investment many times. You are then asked to pay £10,000–£15,000 for a plot of around one-tenth of an acre – enough for a standard house.

This is called 'land-banking' and in theory, it could work. Somewhere in the small print you'll be warned that planning permission is not guaranteed. This is the get-out that ensures the scheme scrapes past the legality test.

But it's such a long shot that so far no one has ever cashed in. The land-bankers pay around £10,000 an acre for the land and rarely have any expertise other than in telling you they can turn the proverbial sow's ear into a silk purse.

Many of these companies have gone bust – the watchdog Financial Services Authority has warned against some of them – leaving investors with a tiny segment of a field, which effectively is worthless as no farmer would want to buy back land from such a large number of individuals – the legal fees would outweigh any benefits. In some cases, investors have not even received legal title to their minuscule slice of rural Britain. Those companies that remain in business have had as little success as those that are no longer alive.

SENSELESS SHARES

Did you or maybe someone in your family ever get a few free shares in a life insurance company or building society that went onto the stockmarket? If you did, the chances are that your name and address are residing on that company's share register – a legal document that all limited companies have to keep, which can be examined by any member of the public.

That makes you a shareholder – and a potential target for a regulated UK-based stockbroker whose main interest will be in taking as much out of your savings (or driving you further into debt) as possible. It's all legal and above board (see box on page 196).

❝ Even if you have just got a few free shares, as a shareholder you are a legal target for stockbrokers keen to get at your savings. ❞

 For more information about what the Financial Services Authority looks into, go to their website: www.fsa.gov.uk and see also page 208.

Enticing shareholders to spend more

Here's how it works:

1 You receive an unsolicited letter inviting you to ask for a 'research report' on the shares of the company you own.

2 You reply with your phone number and signature. You are then giving the company permission to call you.

3 It phones you – ostensibly to ask if you received the material (which, in fact, is usually freely available on the internet and is of low value), but really to ascertain how much money you might have and whether you are prepared to take the risk of buying shares.

4 Instead of being given advice on companies like the mainstream one you own shares in, you'll be persuaded to buy into tiny companies on small stock markets both here and in the United States. You'll be told that you could multiply your money many times.

5 You will not be told that the broker has paid pennies for the shares that you are expected to pay pounds for.

6 You find the expected gains do not materialise.

7 You discover that it is difficult, if not impossible, to sell the shares – even at a loss.

In theory, some small company shares will do amazingly well, some go nowhere and few crash to nothing. The good should outweigh the bad, but Pacific Continental, a company operating in this way and which went bust in summer 2007, rarely made any money for anyone other than its owners as most of its recommendations performed poorly. The veneer of legality here is that you are warned in the small print that small company shares are riskier, may involve you in a loss and may be difficult to sell.

PYRAMID PITCHES

Ever seen one of those flyers that promise '£1,000 a week for just a few hours work'? The chances are they lead to a 'pyramid' scheme where a few will earn a lot and most very little, if anything. But provided the scheme

 For more information about the Pyramid Selling Schemes Regulations, 1989, go to the Office of Public Sector Information website: www.opsi.gov.uk and use the search facility.

adheres to the Pyramid Selling Schemes Regulations 1989, it is legal.

Pyramid schemes work on the basis that the most recently recruited (those at the bottom of the pyramid) sell goods – often cleaning materials or slimming cures – to consumers, sometimes at higher prices than in shops.

There is a small profit in selling these items, although this can involve a lot of work. But the real money is made by recruiting others to sell on your behalf and then getting them to recruit still more people, thus building up your valuable 'downline'.

The end result is that those at the bottom earn little and work hard while those who are in the scheme long enough or who started the scheme earn a lot and work little. The mathematics of individuals in the scheme trying to recruit five more who, in turn, bring in five more each, and so on means you soon run out of potential joiners.

ROTTEN RACING TIPSTERS

Few racing tipsters ever make a profit for very long. And you can get tips for free in many newspapers. So why pay for betting advice?

Some tipsters offer their services either online, via a premium-rate phone call or by post. They back up their claims with lists of past winners.

A number of tipsters do try to make money, in which case they are legal. But according to the Office of Fair Trading, many create these lists after the races are over. The Advertising Standards Authority has criticised a number of tipsters for making promises for what they cannot deliver.

You could lose anything from £50–£10,000 on these schemes. The big losses tend to be when you send money to concerns that offer 'secret computerised programs' to beat the bookies. These do not exist, even if they claim a past history of making a fortune. Nor do the schemes which guarantee you £150 a month forever in return for a total outlay of just £100. These simply cannot work – and never will.

> **❝ There is no such thing as a 'secret computerised program' that will beat the bookies. ❞**

For more information about the work of the Office of fair Trading, go to www.oft.gov.uk. For the Advertising Standards Authority, go to www.asa.org.uk.

Illegal scams

Don't trust what comes into your email inbox, or into your snail-mail box for that matter. You could easily lose big money through the conniving tricks that some people will play.

PHISHING FOR YOUR BANK DETAILS

Have you ever received a 'security alert' from a bank you never deal with or even your own that requests you go to a website and enter details 'to prevent fraud'? This is, in fact, a fraud attempt. It's called phishing (they are fishing for your account details so they can try to empty it – the 'ph' is a reference to 1970s' phenomenon 'phone phreaking'). You can recognise 'phishing' by the tortured English – and because the website you are sent to has no 'www' – it just starts with 'https'.

No real bank ever sends out emails like this. Banks usually shut down phishing sites very quickly, but if you are in doubt (or your account has been compromised), contact your bank at once.

A variation on this is to send out emails pretending to come from Her Majesty's Revenue & Customs (HMRC). These pretend that you are due a tax rebate (often around £100), but to get it you have to send your bank details. Needless to say, there is no rebate and HMRC, which has issued warnings about this, would never send out such emails.

THE DAVID RHODES LETTER

This is the classic chain letter scam – you can see the full text on a number of internet sites. Here 'David Rhodes' (Dave Rhodes in the US version) tells you he was once very poor and now he has a house, a big car and all the trappings of luxury. All you have to do is to send £10 to the name on the top of the list you are supplied with and keep the chain going. It can never work.

WOMEN EMPOWERING WOMEN

This was invented by a man! You persuade seven people to give you £3,000 each 'to help women' and then tell them that because they have joined, they are now allowed to repeat the process themselves. You soon find that recruits are hard to come by – especially as men are barred, cutting out half the population!

66 No real bank ever sends emails requesting security details: this is fraud called 'phishing'. 99

PHONEY JOBS

You receive an email offering you a job with a well-known company with a vague title, such as 'international sales executive'. The job apparently pays a lot of money for very little effort. Eventually, you will be asked for a fee to speed up the process, and, if you send it, another fee until you have nothing left or realise you've been conned. Fraudsters may also ask you for all your bank details, pretending they need it so they can send the money to you, but in reality it is so they can try to empty your account.

An alternative to this is the offer of easy money for helping a well-known computer company with 'software development'.

ADVERTS FOR WORKING AT HOME

These can appear in local giveaway newspapers or convenience shop windows or as flyers through your letterbox. In one version you are promised big money for 'packaging work at home'. The unlikely story is that you will be wrapping difficult shaped parcels. But you have to send money (often about £25) first for 'materials'. You will either get nothing for your money, a few used envelopes or even be sent some old items from a charity shop and told to pack them and send them to an address, which is the last you will ever hear of any money. Mail order firms do not work in this way.

An alternative is to be asked to send money for instructions on 'building your home business'. You send £20 or so. What you get, if anything, is a single piece of paper telling you to repeat the exercise with adverts and sending out the one paragraph instruction sheet informing others to repeat the process.

❝ On the face of it, adverts about working from home look tempting, but beware of sending money in advance of seeing what the 'work' entails. ❞

THE NON-EXISTENT FINE

This one preys on those who have recently been abroad and hired a car. Fraudsters obtain your home address, often from travel company employees, and send you a letter saying you committed a traffic violation in that country. They say that you must send your fine – around £150 – to the address given. It's a post box used by the fraudsters.

THE 'I'LL BUY YOUR CAR FOR MORE THAN YOU WANT' RACKET

People advertising their cars for sale have ended up losing big time. Fraudsters look through classified adverts both online and in print, and then approach sellers, offering them thousands more than they want. The explanation is that the car is in demand in export markets (rarely true because the UK drives on the other side of the road to most other countries). The deal, you are told, is that you can keep half of the excess over what you wanted in return for speeding up the deal.

You are then given a banker's draft for the whole sum. This should be as good as cash. The fraudster takes your car and you pay over the 50 per cent share of the excess.

A few weeks later, your bank tells you the draft is a phoney, so it bounces. But by then, your car and any money you handed over are miles away – and you cannot claim on your theft insurance.

THE PHONEY LOTTERY

Finally, in this section, two of the 'how could anyone be so stupid?' frauds. Sadly, some people are either silly or greedy or both. Fraudsters would not have kept these scams going for so long if there was not a ready queue of victims.

You receive a letter or an email telling you that you have won around £500,000 in a lottery. They usually come from Spain. You may recognise this as a scam because you have never bought a ticket for the draw. But enough people do not see this fact so making

this a paying concept for the criminals behind it.

To get your money, you have to send a 'release fee'. Then, you'll be asked for more until you run out of cash or realise you've been scammed.

THE DEAD DICTATOR'S WIDOW

You receive a letter, email or fax apparently from the widow of a former dictator, or someone who claims to have been the cashier of an international bank, or someone who pretends to be dying from a cancer and suddenly discovers a 'secret life insurance'. The amount of money they have hidden away and which they 'need your help in releasing' is huge – often $35million or $50million. You are offered a 20 per cent slice. You have to send money first, of course. And that's about it. There is no money. But you could lose a lot – some victims who complained have reportedly been the victims of violence.

❝ Fraudsters would not have kept these scams going for so long if sufficient people were not silly or greedy enough to fall for them. ❞

How to spot a scam

Scamsters continually change their spots with new concepts to separate money savers from their cash. But there is really nothing new under the sun – just variations on old themes which, sadly, work.

According to Scambusters, set up by Trading Standards departments and the Office of Fair Trading (see the box at the bottom of page 202), there's a scam out there for everyone. If you let down your guard and think you won't be fooled, you too could become a victim.

Here are some general points to watch out for. Remember that anything that could be too good to be true almost certainly is. Scamsters will:

- Catch you unawares, contacting you, without you asking them to, by phone, email, post or sometimes in person.
- Sound pleasant, well spoken and kind (on the phone or at your door) and want you to think they're your friend.
- Have well designed, professional leaflets and letters.
- Be persistent and persuasive.
- Rush you into making a decision.
- Ask you to send money before you receive their tempting offer or win.
- Ask you to send money straight away.
- Give you a PO box number (or similar device overseas) as their address.
- Not be found easily on the internet.
- Ask you not to tell anyone else about the deal.

New scams from the UK and overseas appear every day, so it is important to know how to spot them. They offer you something for nothing, such as:

- You've won a major prize in a draw or a lottery (even though you haven't entered one).
- An exclusive entry to a scheme that's a sure-fire way to make money.
- A way to earn easy money by helping them get untold millions out of their country.
- The chance to join an investment scheme that will make you huge amounts of money.

There are hundreds of examples but you can protect yourselves by being sceptical. Is it likely that someone you don't know, who has contacted you out of the blue, will give you something for nothing? They'll ask you to:

- Send money up front – an administration fee or tax – the list is endless but it's always a ruse to get you to give them money.
- Give them your bank, credit card or other personal details.

- Ring an expensive premium rate number (all UK premium rate numbers start with 090).
- Buy something to get your prize.

They will lie to you and give you what seem to be good reasons why you should do what they say. They will answer all your objections.

Don't send any money or give any personal details to anyone until you've checked that they are genuine, and talked to a professional or family and friends.

If they ask you to do any of these things, they are trying to cover their tracks and get your money and it's likely to be a scam. Remember ... the tooth fairy does not exist, nor does money grow on trees!

❝ Fraudsters will be able to answer all your objections, but remember that the tooth fairy does not exist and money does not grow on trees! ❞

 To find out more about scams go to the Office of Fair Trading website at www.oft.gov.uk/oft_at_work/consumer_initiatives/scams/.

The money saver's ABC

This chapter gives details on a wide range of sources of further information, giving you help and advice on where to go should anything go wrong.

10

Further information

Consumer and trade organisations offer a huge encyclopedia of free help and advice. Here we point out the most important.

Association of British Credit Unions (ABCUL)

Credit unions offer low-cost loans to those in all walks of life but the movement is primarily aimed at those who would otherwise find it difficult to get credit at normal interest rates. ABCUL is the main trade association for credit unions.

The website tells about services (including savings), how to find a credit union, what you need to do to join or even how to set a new one up yourself. It includes a loan calculator and basic information on financial matters. It also has links to member unions throughout the country.

Association of British Credit Unions
Holyoake House
Hanover Street
Manchester M60 0AS
Tel: 0161 832 3694
www.abcul.org

Association of British Insurers (ABI)

This is the trade body for the UK insurance industry. The association has around 400 companies in membership. Between them, they provide 94 per cent of domestic insurance services sold in the UK.

The website gives information on how insurance works, issues facing insurance companies together with a large number of free consumer guides to subjects ranging from how a small business should cope with flooding to insurance for gay men.

Association of British Insurers
51 Gresham Street
London EC2V 7HQ
Tel: 020 7600 3333
www.abi.org.uk

Association of British Travel Agents (ABTA)

ABTA represents UK travel agents and tour operators responsible for the sale of around over 90 per cent of package holidays and approximately 45 per centof independent travel arrangements. Members operate under a code of conduct to ensure travel arrangements are given with clarity and accuracy.

ABTA checks member finances and has a complaints resolution service backed by a low-cost independent arbitration service. Many arrangements provided by ABTA members are protected in case of the financial failure of the travel company.

ABTA Ltd
68–71 Newman Street
London W1T 3AH
Tel: 020 7637 2444
www.abta.com

Banking Code Standards Board

The board publishes and oversees the banking code, to which all major banks subscribe. It is aimed at ordinary customers including smaller businesses, and the website shows how it affects your dealings with your bank. There are a number of leaflets available while there is also information on how to complain if you feel your bank has transgressed the code.

Banking Code Standards Board
Level 12, City Tower
40 Basinghall Street
London EC2V 5DE
Tel: 0845 230 9694
www.bankingcode.org.uk

British Bankers' Association (BBA)

The BBA is the leading UK banking and financial services trade association. The website is a source of free information for consumers that ranges from identity checks to how disability law affects banks and their relationships with customers.

British Bankers' Association
Pinners Hall
105–108 Old Broad Street
London EC2N 1EX
Tel: 020 7216 8800
www.bba.org.uk

Building Societies Association (BSA)

The BSA is the trade association for the UK's mutually owned home loans and savings firms. The website has listings for its members across the country and links to their own websites, information on topics, ranging from fraud to how to re-unite yourself with lost savings, and what makes a mutual building society different from a shareholder-owned bank.

Building Societies Association
6th Floor, York House
23 Kingsway
London WC2B 6UJ
Tel: 020 7437 0655
Consumer information: 020 7437 0655 (ask for BSA Consumer Line)
www.bsa.org.uk

Callcredit

Callcredit is one of the UK's three consumer credit reference agencies with an extensive range of information for individuals as well as businesses. You can order a copy of your credit reference file on the website – there is a statutory service for £2 but also a number of enhanced services if you wish to check your file often or instantly online.

Callcredit Ltd
One Park Lane
Leeds
West Yorkshire LS3 1EP
Tel: 0113 244 1555
www.callcredit.co.uk or
www.mycallcredit.com

CIFAS

CIFAS is the UK's financial fraud prevention service with 270 members spread across banking, credit cards, asset finance, retail credit, mail order, insurance, telecommunications, savings and investments, factoring and share dealing.

The website has information on fraud, how to fight it and how to complain if you are a victim. It tells you how to register for the protective registration service – worth considering if you have been the victim of a mugging or burglary and personal identification documents have been stolen. There is a risk they could be used by the thief to obtain credit or other products and services fraudulently in your name.

CIFAS
4th Floor, Central House
14 Upper Woburn Place
London WC1H 0NN
No public telephone
www.cifas.org.uk

Citizens Advice Bureau (CAB)

This is the national association that links the free-to-use CAB throughout the country. The Citizens Advice service helps people resolve their legal, money and other problems by providing free information and advice from over 3,000 locations, and by influencing policymakers. Citizens Advice and each Citizens Advice Bureau are registered charities reliant on over 20,000 volunteers helping people to resolve nearly 5.5 million problems every year.

The website has information on your local CAB for whom you should turn for advice as the central Citizens Advice does not deal directly with the public.

Find your local office from the telephone directory or go to website: www.citizensadvice.org.uk/

Consumer Credit Counselling Service (CCCS)

The CCCS is a registered charity whose purpose is to assist people who are in financial difficulty by providing free, independent, impartial and realistic advice. It provides advice on personal budgeting, how to use credit and, where appropriate, managing achievable plans to repay debts. The CCCS does not charge fees to consumers.

Consumer Credit Counselling Service
Wade House
Merrion Centre
Leeds LS2 8NG
Tel: 0800 138 1111
www.cccs.co.uk

Consumer Direct

Consumer Direct is the Office of Fair Trading's call centre where you can get advice on consumer problems free of charge. It can help before you buy, tell you how to handle rogue tradespeople and stores, give tips on buying items such as second-hand cars, computers, washing machine repairs, and help with any disputes that arise. It works in partnership with local trading standards officers – it is intended as a one-stop shop wherever you live or work so you don't have to find the local council trading standards department or worry about if it is interested in your problem (trading standards departments differ in their priorities and budgets). But it does not offer legal advice or help with financial transactions.

Tel: 08454 04 05 06 (8am–6:30pm, Monday–Friday; 9am–1pm, Saturday) www.consumerdirect.gov.uk

Council of Mortgage Lenders

This is a trade association for firms involved in mortgage lending. It does not deal directly with the public, but its website has a range of general consumer information, including downloadable guides on home buying and selling, equity release products, buy-to-let products and mortgage payment protection insurance. There is also a list of FAQs about mortgages and the mortgage market, and a mortgage calculator and repayment tables for consumers wishing to work out mortgage costs. While the Council is not involved in complaints, it does offer information on how to complain about mortgage companies.

Council of Mortgage Lenders
Bush House
North West Wing
Aldwych
London WC2B 4PJ
Tel: 0845 373 6771
Consumer information: 020 7438 8956
www.cml.org.uk/cml/consumers

Equifax

This is one of the three consumer credit reference agencies used by lenders and others who need to check your status. It gives information on understanding your credit report and what to do if you believe there is a mistake. You can apply for a copy of your credit report online for £11.95 or for £2 by post. Alternatively, you can sign up for regular updates for £7.50 a month.

Equifax
Capital House
25 Chapel Street
London NW1 5DS
No public telephone
www.equifax.co.uk

Experian

This is one of three major credit reference agencies whose data can determine whether you are accepted or not for a loan and, if accepted, whether this is at the standard or a higher interest rate. You can apply for a copy of your report online or send £2 to:

Experian
Talbot House
Talbot Street
Nottingham NG80 1TH
Tel: 0115 941 0888
but call 0870 241 6212 to discuss credit reports
www.experian.co.uk

Family Law

This is an association of solicitors specialising in family law such as divorce, adoption, neighbour disputes and making a will. The Family Law website directs you to a local member. There is also an email enquiry form.

Family Law
Interactive Law
Scorrier Park
Scorrier
Redruth
Cornwall TR16 5AU
Tel: 01209 822060
www.family-solicitors.co.uk

Financial Ombudsman Service (FOS)

The FOS is a free service that resolves disputes between consumers and financial companies. It is used when the relationship between the customer and the company has broken down. The service's decision is binding on the company but consumers can take the matter to court if they wish.

The website has free fact sheets on topics including payment protection insurance and endowment mortgages, and tells you how and when to complain.

The Financial Ombudsman Service
South Quay Plaza
183 Marsh Wall
London E14 9SR
Tel: 020 7964 1000
www.financial-ombudsman.org.uk

Financial Services Authority (FSA)

The FSA is the regulator of almost all financial transactions, including savings, investments, loans and insurances, but not property transactions.

The consumer section of its website explains financial basics, giving more detail on individual products, and has links to unbiased tables covering many money areas. You can check the status of an adviser and look at recent press releases, warnings to consumers and find out how companies are regulated.

Financial Services Authority
25 The North Colonnade
Canary Wharf
London E14 5HS
Tel: 020 7066 1000
Consumer helpline (including Central Register authorisation queries):
0845 606 1234
You can order leaflets on:
0845 456 1555 or download them from the website:
www.moneymadeclear.fsa.gov.uk

Help the Aged

Help the Aged is a charity that researches the needs of older people in the UK and overseas and campaigns for changes in policy. It provides community services and publishes information for the elderly (and those who are responsible for them) on finance and how to stay healthy as well as guidance on choosing a care home.

Help the Aged
207–221 Pentonville Road
London N1 9UZ
Tel: 020 7278 1114
www.helptheaged.org.uk

Her Majesty's Courts Service (HMCS)

HMCS is an executive agency of the Ministry of Justice. Its remit is to deliver justice effectively and efficiently to the public. It is responsible for managing the magistrates' courts, the Crown Court, county courts, the High Court and Court of Appeal in England and Wales. The website has a wide range of information including where to find a court, forms to fill in, dealing with the small claims procedure (including issuing proceedings), divorce proceedings and civil partnership dissolution, wills and probate and other forms of court hearings.

Her Majesty's Courts Service
Ministry of Justice
Selborne House
54 Victoria Street
London
Tel: 020 7210 8500
www.hmcourts-service.gov.uk/

Her Majesty's Revenue & Customs (HMRC)

HMRC deals with all forms of taxes, including income tax, capital gains tax, inheritance tax, and with tax credits, national insurance, VAT and stamp duty on property purchases.

The website is not one of the easiest to navigate but it has almost everything that HMRC has ever put in the public realm. It gives details of local offices and of its large number of helplines, which offer aid with everything from inheritance tax to reporting tax evasion as well as help with your own tax matters.

HMRC
Somerset House
Strand
London WC2R 1LB
Tel: 0845 900 0444 (income tax line – there are many others)
www.hmrc.gov.uk

IFA Promotion (IFAP)

This is a commercial organisation that will help you find an independent financial adviser. Consumer guides covering areas such as school fees planning, endowments, ethical investment and offshore finance are also on its website.

Consumer hotline: 0800 085 3250
www.unbiased.co.uk
www.impartial.co.uk (the IFAP mortgage broker specialist)

Information Commissioner's Office (ICO)

The UK's independent authority that promotes access to official information and protects personal information. It gives advice on getting official information, dealing with unwanted sales calls and spam email, and how to find out environmental information from official sources. It also tells you how to make complaints about data intrusion.

The Information Commissioner's Office
Wycliffe House
Water Lane
Wilmslow
Cheshire SK9 5AF
Tel: 01625 54 57 45
www.ico.gov.uk

The Law Society

This is the professional association for solicitors in England and Wales. It offers information about how to find a lawyer and gives access to information about the legal profession. Complaints are dealt with by the Legal Complaints Service (see below). Postal enquires to:

The Law Society
Ipsley Court
Berrington Close
Worcestershire B98 0TD
Tel: 020 7242 1222
www.lawsociety.org.uk

Legal Complaints Service

This deals with complaints against solicitors over areas such as professional misconduct, conflict of interest and overcharging. The website details the procedure, starting with a complaint to the firm involved and leading up to possible compensation. When contacting the service with a definitive problem, you should be able to send copies of all documentation.

Legal Complaints Service
Victoria Court
8 Dormer Place
Leamington Spa
Warwickshire CV32 5AE
Tel: 0845 608 6565
www.legalcomplaints.org.uk

National Debtline

This is a free advice service with a national telephone helpline for people with debt problems in England, Scotland and Wales. The service is free, confidential and independent.

The National Debtline is a registered charity and provides self-help advice to callers and has written self-help packs and factsheets to back this up. It can also help callers with the setting up of debt management plans. The website has a large number of factsheets that you can download for free.

National Debtline
The Arch
48–52 Floodgate Street
Birmingham B5 5SL
Tel: 0808 808 4000
www.nationaldebtline.co.uk

National Rail Enquiries

This is a website giving railway timetable and ticket cost information across Great Britain. It has links to each of the train-operating companies and gives live updates on problems and difficulties across the network.

Tel: 08457 48 49 50
www.nationalrail.co.uk

Office of Fair Trading (OFT)

The OFT is responsible for making markets work well for consumers by promoting and protecting consumer interests throughout the UK, while ensuring that businesses are fair and competitive.

Enquires should generally be sent to Consumer Direct (see pages 206–7) as the OFT does not deal directly with consumers or businesses.

Office of Fair Trading
Fleetbank House
2–6 Salisbury Square
London EC4Y 8JX
Tel: 020 7211 8000
www.oft.gov.uk

The Pension Service

This is part of the Department for Work and Pensions, set up to improve pension services both for existing and future pensioners. It has a network of local pension centres with links on its website. It will also work out the amount of state pension and pension credit that you are entitled to, provides a face-to-face information service if requested, and give other general pension information.

Tel: 0845 60 60 265 (0845 60 60 275 for Welsh-speaking customers living in Wales) (8am–8pm, Monday–Friday)
www.thepensionservice.gov.uk

The Pensions Advisory Service

This is an independent, non-profit organisation that provides free information, advice and guidance on the whole spectrum of pensions, covering state, company and personal pensions and stakeholder schemes.

The Pensions Advisory Service
11 Belgrave Road
London SW1V 1RB
Tel: 0845 601 2923
www.pensionsadvisoryservice.org.uk

TaxAid

This is a UK charity providing free tax advice to people who cannot afford to pay a professional adviser. The service is independent and confidential. It can help anyone on a low income, whether employed, self-employed, retired or on benefits, who cannot afford to pay for professional advice. It also helps you understand your rights and responsibilities under the UK tax system, including the information HMRC have sent you about your tax, on matters such as PAYE, self-assessment, tax credits and allowances, and tax for the self-employed. It will also help you if you are worried because you are the subject of an HMRC enquiry; you cannot pay your tax and may be facing legal proceedings for non-payment; you think you should get a tax refund; or you feel you are being unfairly treated by the HMRC. All TaxAid advisers are qualified tax professionals.

TaxAid
Room 304
Linton House
164–180 Union Street
London SE1 0LH
Tel: 0845 120 3779 (10am–12 noon, Monday–Thursday)
www.taxaid.org.uk

Transport for London (TfL)

TfL is London's transport network. The website has information on travelling in the capital including public transport (underground, overground, buses and Thames river boats), cycling, congestion charge, Oyster cards and ticketing, dial-a-ride (for those with disabilities), walking and how to get from one place to another using journey planners. There is live travel news as well as updates on services and cancellations.

Transport for London
23rd Floor Empress State Building
Empress Approach
London SW6 1TR
Tel: 020 7222 1234
www.tfl.gov.uk

Which? Legal Services

This comes from Which?. It offers unlimited professional legal advice from lawyers for a subscription, advising you directly on a wide range of problems, which involve:

- Consumer law – problems with goods and services
- Employment law
- Holiday problems
- Neighbour disputes
- Parking, speeding and clamping fines
- Probate administration.

Membership hotline: 0800 252 100
www.whichlegalservice.co.uk

Index

Index

Index

Which? is the leading independent consumer champion in the UK.
A not-for-profit organisation, we exist to make individuals as powerful as the organisations they deal with in everyday life. The next few pages give you a taster of our many products and services. For more information, log onto www.which.co.uk or call 0800 252 100.

Which? Online

www.which.co.uk gives you access to all Which? content online and much, much more. It's updated regularly, so you can read hundreds of product reports and Best Buy recommendations, keep up to date with Which? campaigns, compare products, use our financial planning tools and interactive car-buying guide. You can also access all the reviews from *The Which? Good Food Guide*, ask an expert in our interactive forums, register for email updates and browse our online shop – so what are you waiting for? To subscribe, go to www.which.co.uk.

Which? Legal Service

Which? Legal Service offers immediate access to first-class legal advice at unrivalled value. One low-cost annual subscription allows members to enjoy unlimited legal advice by telephone on a wide variety of legal topics, including consumer law – problems with goods and services, employment law, holiday problems, neighbour disputes, parking, speeding and clamping fines and probate administration. To subscribe, call the membership hotline: 0800 252 100 or go to www.whichlegalservice.co.uk.

Which? Money

Whether you want to boost your pension, make your savings work harder or simply need to find the best credit card, *Which? Money* has the information you need. *Which? Money* offers you honest, unbiased reviews of the best (and worst) new personal finance deals, from bank accounts to loans, credit cards to savings accounts. Throughout the magazine you will find saving tips and ideas to make your budget go further plus dozens of Best Buys. To subscribe, go to www.whichmoney.magazine.co.uk.

Which? Books

Which? Books

Other books in this series

Baby and Toddler Essentials

Anne Smith
ISBN: 978 1 84490 035 0
Price £10.99

Knowing what you need to buy when you have a child or grandchild can be a daunting business – the choice is huge, the laws are complicated and it's important to get it right. Taking each area of equipment in turn from birth to toys for your toddler, *Baby and Toddler Essentials* explores the goods on the market and identifies the products that might help, the products to avoid, and the essentials you really can't live without.

CV and Interview Handbook

Sue Tumelty
ISBN: 978 1 84490 047 3
Price £10.99

Changing jobs or embarking on a new career can be one of life's stressful events. This guide looks at the all-important CV, how to interpret job adverts, what you should and shouldn't say in a job interview and much more. *CV and Interview Handbook* takes you through the job-hunting process from application to assessment centres and your first week at work.

Making a Civil Claim

Melanie McDonald
ISBN: 978 1 84490 037 4
Price £10.99

Making a Civil Claim is the first law book in the *Essential Guides* series and is essential reading for anyone involved in a dispute and who may be facing court or even a trial. It covers small claims as well as fast-track and multi-track cases and explains everything from organising your documents and making sure all the available evidence is in place, to finding the right solicitor or barrister for your case.

Which? Books

Which? Books provide impartial, expert advice on everyday matters from finance to law, property to major life events. We also publish the country's most trusted restaurant guide, *The Which? Good Food Guide*. To find out more about Which? Books, log on to www.which.co.uk or call 01903 828557.

❝ Which? tackles the issues that really matter to consumers and gives you the advice and active support you need to buy the right products. **❞**